This is the
DOBERMAN PINSCHER

by **Louise Ziegler Spirer**
and **Evelyn Miller**

Photography by Louise Van der Meid
Drawings by Ernest Hart

Distributed in the U.S.A. by T.F.H. Publications, Inc., 211 West Sylvania Avenue, P.O. Box 27, Neptune City, N.J. 07753; in England by T.F.H. (Gt. Britain) Ltd., 13 Nutley Lane, Reigate, Surrey; in Canada to the book store and library trade by Clarke, Irwin & Company, Clarwin House, 791 St. Clair Avenue West, Toronto 10, Ontario; in Canada to the pet trade by Rolf C. Hagen Ltd., 3225 Sartelon Street, Montreal 382, Quebec; in Southeast Asia by Y.W. Ong, 9 Lorong 36 Geylang, Singapore 14; in Australia and the south Pacific by Pet Imports Pty. Ltd., P.O. Box 149, Brookvale 2100, N.S.W., Australia. Published by T.F.H. Publications Inc., Ltd., The British Crown Colony of Hong Kong.

ISBN 0-87666-282-1

Acknowledgements

Special thanks are due to Girleen Kenny, Herbert F. Spirer and Matthew A. Kenny for invaluable assistance in the editing, typing, and checking that went into the preparation of this book. The advice of Jack Patterson, D.V.M., has been gratefully received, and we have endeavored to live up to his high standards. The latest official Doberman Pinscher standards were supplied to us by the Doberman Pinscher Club of America.

Photography Acknowledgements

The authors wish to express their appreciation to Mrs. Louise Brown Van der Meid and Mr. Ernest Hart for their help in illustrating this book. They also wish to thank the following people who allowed their Doberman Pinschers to be photographed: Mr. and Mrs. Barney Hayden, Mr. Ben Brown (Professional Handler), Mrs. Viola Hoskins, Mr. Daniel Heredia (Professional Handler), Mr. and Mrs. Dino DiPrimio, Mrs. Ivan E. Gilbert, Jack and Cecile Harris, Mrs. Carol Dougherty, Mrs. Dorothy Ormiston, Mrs. R. C. Dickson (Groomer), and Robert Ormiston and Chris Gilbert (Models).

CONTENTS

This is the
DOBERMAN PINSCHER

Introduction

At last you have the dog of your dreams. Today is the day you bring home your purebred Doberman Pinscher.

You have consulted with the experts, visited dog shows, examined many litters of purebred Dobermans, and finally found the puppy *you* want. And here he is—home with you. He's probably scared and lonely for his mother, brothers and sisters, uncertain about his new master, hungry and tired. You too may be uncertain. You are now responsible for this small bundle of flesh and blood—responsible for his care, housing, training, grooming, feeding, and health. You are now responsible to both yourself and your neighbors for a well-trained, healthy, and happy dog.

Welcome the Doberman puppy with all the courtesy and care his excellent breeding deserves.

Be prepared, and have a dog bed waiting for the puppy when you bring him home.

If you purchase a puppy, give him plenty of love. He misses the members of the litter from which he was purchased.

If you have decided on an adult Doberman, give him all of your attention until you have earned his loyalty.

Welcome your dog, show him his bed, offer him a little warm milk or formula (if you received some from the kennel), and cuddle him a little. Soon you will be sure of each other, and good friends.

Your dog's breeder has spent many hours studying Dobermans and scientifically breeding them to obtain the best possible dogs. He has been careful with their diet and kennel care. But no amount of heredity and no amount of very early care can make up for what *you* must do to rear a healthy dog. This book is intended to offer helps and hints for the care of your dog, and we suggest you read it through carefully. It will guide you through the many phases of dog life. This is a practical book for you, the dog owner; it makes no claim to offer instant cures and sure-fire solutions to your every problem.

In the meantime, enjoy your dog. He is one of the most elegant of the canine world. His breeding, carriage, and handsome coloring set him apart among dogs. The Doberman is known to be a one-man dog, but his gentleness and protective attitude towards children and his quality as a guardian make him an ideal addition to your household. Kindly treated and well cared for, he will always be a pleasure.

Chapter I
History

The dog has been man's best friend for many thousands of years. He has not only been his friend but his guardian, sentry, sheepherder and messenger boy as well. The dog's intelligence and loyalty have served man well and in return, man has taken care of his pet—fed and housed him, written and sung songs about him, and painted his picture.

ANCIENT HISTORY

The ancient dog was closely related to the wolf. They had common ancestors and their tooth structure, for example, is alike. Dogs hunted cooperatively in packs, as wolves have always done, using their cunning and physical strength to run down game. Soon after man and dog had joined forces, there were already several distinct dog types, such as the Hound, Mastiff and Shepherd. The wolf was left behind to develop his own family history.

Our earliest pictured dog was portrayed in the oldest paintings ever found, the cave paintings of Southern France, dating back 50,000 years. The dogs depicted appear to be of a Shepherd or Alsatian type.

Dog remains have been found in neolithic England; others resembling Samoyeds were found in cold climates; Elkhounds were living in Scandinavia 6,000 years ago, obviously companions and hunters for the Vikings.

In the Near East, archeologists have found seals showing Mastiff-like hounds in the diggings. Fortunately, the ancient Egyptians left complete records in their tombs and temples, and the dog was obviously used for work or hunting. Kings were often shown hunting with their pack of hounds—Bassets or Mastiffs or perhaps Terriers. They also used dogs to guard their flocks and as war dogs.

The glorious heritage the Greeks left in art, literature and architecture also includes dogs. Homer tells of the dog "Argus" in the *Odyssey*, and one of the earliest Greek paintings ever found shows a group of palace maidens in a chariot, preceded by a young man with a large dog resembling a Saluki hound.

12

An early story about dogs concerns the Grecian city of Corinth. Dogs were let loose to patrol the shoreline. One night an enemy attacked the city. A massacre of Corinth was averted when the dog sentries attacked the invaders and held them off until the alarm had been sounded.

By Roman times there were six fairly distinct classes of dogs— shepherds such as Huskies and Chows, scent hounds (the Romans hunted with Bloodhounds); Greyhounds like the Saluki and Afghan, sporting or Spaniel types like the Setter, Retriever or Poodle; and dogs used for war purposes such as the Bulldog, Great Dane, and Boxer. The Romans kept housedogs in their homes for pets, most likely mongrels or perhaps pet toy dogs. Naturally, these different types of dogs were not purebred in today's sense, but they closely resembled their modern descendents.

HISTORY OF THE DOBERMAN PINSCHER

But the Doberman Pinscher is a truly modern dog, first noted in the 1880's, although his ancestors were undoubtedly found in olden times. Despite this newness, however, his true origins are shrouded in mystery. The Doberman was probably first bred in one of the picture postcard towns in the province of Thuringia, Germany. Because travel was slow and limited, areas often developed their own types of dogs as a result of constant inbreeding.

We do know that in Apolda, Germany, in 1880, Louis Dobermann, night watchman, sometime city official and dog fancier, had several dogs resembling the Doberman which he used to help him with his work. He must have needed an alert, fearless dog in his rounds, and he probably bred animals which caught his fancy and met his needs as well.

The first serious breeder on record was Otto Goeller. He was one of the earliest to recognize the quality of our dog and to breed him for specific characteristics. Goeller was so enthusiastic about Dobermans that the neighbors soon complained of the noise and he was forced to send some of his dogs away. The first Dobermann-pinscherklub in Apolda was founded by Goeller in 1899. One year later the Doberman was officially accepted as a new breed in Germany. Black and tan were the only allowed colors at that time.

Although we cannot exactly pinpoint our dog's ancestors, we can, judging by the appearance, guess at the ingredients.

The chief influences appear to be the early German Shepherd (unlike today's modern German Shepherd), the Rottweiler butcher's dog, some German Shorthaired Pointer, perhaps a pinch of Weimaraner. Some dog connoisseurs claim that the Manchester Black-and-Tan Terrier was an important contributor. Certainly the colorings are similar. In addition, the word *pinscher* means *terrier* in German.

Does this sound as if your handsome modern dog is a mongrel? Certainly not! Remember that all dogs began as mixtures and were gradually sorted out. Dogs were bred for appearance and utility and breeders tried to duplicate any trait that seemed desirable and to eliminate poor qualities. At first, this was done mostly by trial and error, but today modern breeders, with their knowledge of heredity and complete records of each dog's ancestors, can breed scientifically for better and finer dogs.

As soon as the Doberman was recognized, only purebred dogs were mated and we now have complete records from almost the first purebred dog on down to today's fine Doberman families.

There is some German Shorthaired Pointer "blood" in the Doberman Pinscher.

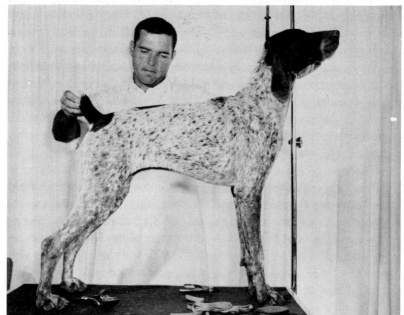

Of all the breeds, the German Shepherd's influence is the greatest in the Doberman of today. Photo by Three Lions, Inc.

FOREIGN HISTORY

Germany

The Doberman originated in Germany (the Germans spell the name with two n's—Dobermannpinscher) and is, naturally, very popular there. The first club was formed in 1899 and standards were set up. By 1900 the dog was accepted as a *bona fide* breed in Germany and shown in many dog shows. The Cologne Dog Show in 1910 lists 105 Doberman entries.

Many of the most illustrious Doberman champions were bred in Germany and most of the dogs today have some ancestors dating back to these early German dogs.

During both World Wars the Germans used the Doberman as a war dog. Although breeding suffered as a result of wartime hardships, there has recently been renewed interest.

Holland

By 1909 the Doberman had emigrated to Holland and many people immediately bought and bred them. They were even exported to the Dutch East Indies where they flourished despite the climate. You can still find Doberman Pinscher clubs there.

Switzerland

The Swiss were also interested in the Doberman and the first club was formed there in 1902. For a while, because of some rather rowdy dogs, many people were reluctant to buy these dogs, but careful breeding and training soon erased this strain. The Swiss were attracted to the Doberman because of his adaptability to the weather and the shorthaired coat which dried quickly and held no odor. One of their famous dams, Miss Bernecki, whelped many litters which went on to fame and fortune.

Other countries such as Austria, France, Belgium and Italy soon founded clubs with many ardent admirers, as did England.

MODERN HISTORY OF THE DOBERMAN

The Doberman was intended as a working dog—to be used for guard work, sentry duty, shepherding and also as a watch dog. We doubt if people at home use their Dobermans to herd sheep, but they certainly can be fine watch dogs and protectors of hearth and home.

Many Dobermans, however, are trained by the police and military as guard dogs and war dogs.

A champion Doberman Pinscher female owned by Mrs. J. M. Stebbins, Jr. Photo by Orlando, from Three Lions.

Experts feel that there is a pinch of Weimaraner in today's Doberman.
Photo by Three Lions.

Perhaps the Doberman is best known for his work with the armed forces. With his intelligence, alertness and physical prowess, he can be easily trained for such work.

We have evidence that the ancient Assyrians, Persians, Greeks and Romans used war dogs. By 1910 the British were training dogs for both sentry and rescue work. The Germans, using both Dobermans and German Shepherds, had 6,000 dogs in service by 1914.

The Doberman performed many heroic tasks during his war service, but perhaps his most important activity was rescuing the wounded. There is evidence that at least 4,000 soldiers were first found by trained dogs. The dogs were taught that if they found a man in a prone position, they were to go back to their masters and lead him to the wounded man.

Dogs were even used to find enemy positions. The U.S. Marine Corps has reason to be proud of its K-9 dog corps, the "Devil Dogs."

An outstanding best in show winner, Ch. Dortmund Delly's Colonel Jet, is also a leading sire. Photo by Wm. Brown.

Six dogs, four of them Dobermans, were cited for their work in the South Pacific. These dogs "hit the beach" with the Marines.

"Andy" saved a Marine tank platoon by locating the Japanese gun nests which were harassing the group. "Otto" and "Rex" warned their masters of Japanese snipers and located their gun positions. Many of our boys were saved by these fearless dogs!

But the Doberman is equally at home in less war-like places. Some are used as seeing-eye dogs, others as night watchmen, but most are family dogs. Unfortunately, because of his war work, the Doberman is sometimes feared. As every Doberman owner knows, this is far from the truth. Your Doberman has more than his share of the qualities of "man's best friend." Affectionate, fond of children, playful and loyal, and with great intelligence, he is a perfect member of the household.

THE DOBERMAN IN AMERICA

The Doberman Pinscher emigrated to the United States early in the twentieth century. Among the early breeders were Mr. Jaeger of Rochester, Mr. and Mrs. Herman Meyer of Philadelphia and Mr. and Mrs. Vucassovitch in Boston. These devoted Doberman Pinscher fanciers began breeding their dogs soon after they arrived here, and their kennels were known throughout the country. The Doberman Pinscher Club of America was started by Mr. George H. Earle III in 1922.

By 1923, the Westminster Dog Show, America's most important show, had asked Peter Umlauff, a well-known authority, to judge Doberman entries. Among the leading dogs at that time were sons and daughters of such outstanding German champions as Alto v. Sigalsburg and Helios v. Siegestor. These dogs produced lines which included over 200 champions, many of whom were brought to America.

In recent years the Glenhugel Kennels and Pontchartrain Kennels owned by the outstanding breeder, Glenn S. Staines, have produced champion Dobermans.

At last report there were more than 7,400 Dobermans in competition. Eighty-four champions are credited. There are more than 3,000 registrations a year, and the Doberman ranks 23rd in registrations.

Ch. Rancho Dobe's Storm is an outstanding winner, having won

Best in Show at the Westminster Dog Show twice in a row, surely a signal honor. Other important champions are Ch. Dictator v. Glenhugel and Ch. Delegate v. d. Elbe. Two famous sires are Ch. Dortmund Delly's Colonel Jet and Ch. Brown's Eric. On the distaff side, Ch. Jessy v. d. Sonnenhoehe and Meadowmist Isis of Ahrtal are busy as champion mothers as well as show winners.

It is interesting to see that one of the more recent winners, Borong the Tonga, was sired by Dortmund Delly's Colonel Jet.

America has also used Dobermans extensively in police work. For example, police dogs are used around hospitals to prevent muggings. The Baltimore police claim that one dog equals six men. Their K-9 Corps has 400 dogs (at last count) which are credited with over 500 arrests. A Dobe "on duty" will patrol his area and if he senses someone lurking, will hold him at bay until his master arrives. Such a dog will attack only in self-defense or upon command from his trainer.

A large city department store, plagued with after-hours robberies, uses trained Dobermans to patrol the aisles. Thefts were cut down tremendously after word got around.

Dogs like the Doberman can even be employed to find lost children. Police give the dog a piece of the child's clothing and this is enough for the dog to get the scent. Criminals are also tracked the same way.

CHARACTERISTICS WHICH HISTORY BRED

In later chapters the physical and mental characteristics of the Doberman will be discussed in detail. But one thing we should note: breeds of dogs didn't just grow like Topsy. Dog owners liked certain types of dogs for certain reasons and because of this, purebreds were encouraged. In this way they could be assured of traits and appearance. The early Dobermans were used as watch dogs. Several breeds contributed characteristics to the original Doberman strain which were encouraged. The Rottweiler butcher dogs were strong, alert dogs used to herd and guard cattle. This physical strength was much admired by the townspeople of Thuringia, Germany.

Although there is some dispute about this, the coloration of the Manchester Black-and-Tan Terrier was much admired and probably bred into the Doberman for this reason early in his development.

As we noted before, the lack of rapid transportation in Germany at this time caused much inbreeding. It was easy, therefore, for certain types of dogs to be developed quickly. Dobermann, Goeller and other local breeders soon recognized the value of this new breed —his colorings and physical beauty and mental alertness were much in demand—and they bred into the Doberman many of his fine modern-dog qualities.

Chapter II
Description

When you first went out looking for a dog, did you know that you wanted a Doberman Pinscher?

Many people see a dog in a store window, and he is such a cute puppy that they immediately dash off and buy one just like him, or even buy that "doggy in the window."

Others come to like a dog they see in someone's house and ask where they can get a similar one. Or, if one of the dogs in the neighborhood has a litter of puppies, you will often see some of her children in nearby houses (even though most people prefer to send their look-alikes to other areas).

Still others, scientific in their selection of a dog, go to the library and look up different breeds of dogs, or write to the American Kennel

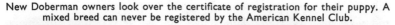

New Doberman owners look over the certificate of registration for their puppy. A mixed breed can never be registered by the American Kennel Club.

Club for advice and information. Or they may find their dog through magazines about dogs which advertise puppies for sale.

While you may have obtained him through any of these means, your Doberman Pinscher is not a common dog—you just won't find him on every street corner or in many homes. Nor are there as many breeders or kennels as for the more popular breeds such as the Poodle or Cocker Spaniel. The Dobe has very special qualities, and you will want to know what your Doberman is like, temperamentally and physically.

The Doberman is a dog of middle size, powerful and muscular. He needs adequate space to keep him in tone and lots of protein to maintain his powerful body. His outstanding feature is his proud, elegant carriage, reflecting nobility and alertness. He is fearless and loyal and is, for the most part, a devoted family dog. He will protect your home and family.

The Doberman is unusual for his utility. Many of today's pure-breds are not used for the work their ancestors did. Dogs were, after all, bred for work as well as companionship, and many dogs had to work on farms or act as guards or draft animals.

The Doberman is no exception. His forebears were sentries, guards, sheep-herders, and war dogs, and the modern Doberman is still used for this type of work. His most famous use is that of police and war dog. As a guard or sentry he has served man for many generations. In crowded cities the police use dogs to control crowds or as patrols in lonely parks and streets. Department stores employ the Doberman as night watchmen. Such a well-trained dog can terrorize a prowler or thief should one attempt to burglarize this dog's territory. Because of his usefulness, breeders have encouraged these characteristics in the breed.

AKC STANDARD

The American Kennel Club sets the standards for all breeds of pedigreed dogs in America. No dog can be the complete ideal, but show winners are generally those dogs which come closest to the ideal. If you are buying a dog for show purposes, it is wise to check the points you need. Even if you just want a dog for the home, you may still want to purchase a dog which conforms closely to the standards, for some day you may wish to have a litter. Selecting your dog carefully also discourages those unscrupulous breeders who are turning out dogs with little regard for the quality of the breed.

A *fault* is a departure from the ideal. It is not enough to disqualify a dog from the show ring, but it hurts his chances of winning.

A *disqualifying fault* disqualifies a dog from showing. It is of a more serious nature than a fault.

The standard by which the Doberman is judged was drawn up by the Doberman Pinscher Club of America and approved by the Board of Directors of the American Kennel Club, as follows:

General conformation and appearance: The appearance is that of a dog of good middle size, with a body that is square, the height measured vertically from the ground to the highest point of the withers, equaling the length, measured horizontally, from the forechest to the rear projection of the upper thigh. Height at the withers— males, 26-28 inches—the ideal is about 27 inches; bitches, 24-26 inches—the ideal is about $25\frac{1}{2}$ inches. The Doberman is compactly built, muscular and powerful, built for great endurance and speed. He is elegant in appearance, of proud carriage, reflecting great nobility and temperament. He is energetic, watchful, determined, alert, fearless, loyal, and obedient.

Faults: Coarseness. Fine Greyhound build. Undersized or oversized.

Disqualifying Faults: Shyness, viciousness. A dog shall be judged fundamentally shy if, refusing to stand for examination, it shrinks away from the judge; if it fears an approach from the rear; if it shies at sudden and unusual noises to a marked degree. A dog that attacks, or attempts to attack, either the judge or handler, is definitely vicious. An aggressive or belligerent attitude toward other dogs shall not be deemed viciousness.

HEAD

Head Shape; Long and dry, resembling a blunt wedge, both frontal and profile views. When seen from the front the head widens gradually toward the base of the ears in a practically unbroken line. Top of skull is flat, turning with a slight stop to bridge of muzzle, with muzzle line extending parallel to the top line of the skull. Cheeks are flat and muscular. The lips lie close to the jaws and are not drooping. The jaws are full and powerful, well filled under the eyes. The nose is solid black in black dogs, dark brown in brown ones, and dark gray in blues.

Faults: The head out of proportion to body. Ram's, dishfaced, cheeky or snipey heads.

Eyes; Almond-shaped, not round, moderately deep set, not prominent, with vigorous energetic expression. The iris is of uniform color, ranging from medium to darkest brown in black dogs, the darker shade being the more desirable. In reds or blues, the color of the iris should blend with that of the markings, but not be of a lighter hue than that of the markings.

Faults: Light eyes, slit eyes, glassy eyes.

Teeth; Strongly developed and white. Lower incisors upright and touching inside of upper incisors—a true scissors bite. Forty-two teeth (22 in lower jaw, 20 in upper jaw). Distemper teeth should not be penalized.

Disqualifying Faults: Overshot more than 3/16 of an inch; undershot more than $\frac{1}{8}$ of an inch.

Ears; Well-trimmed and carried erect. (In all states where ear trimming is prohibited or where dogs with cropped ears cannot be shown, the foregoing requirements are waived.) The upper attachment of the ears, when held erect, should be on a level with the top of the skull.

Ch. Haydenhills Brian of Catharden, owned by Mrs. Hayden.

26

Front view of good male Doberman head.

Neck; Carried upright, well-muscled, and dry. Well arched, with nape of neck widening gradually toward body. Length of neck proportionate to body and head.

BODY

Back; Short, firm, of sufficient width, and muscular at the loin, extending in a straight line from withers to the slightly rounded croup.

Withers; Pronounced and forming the highest point of body.

Brisket; Full and broad, reaching deep to the elbow.

Chest; Broad; forechest well defined.

Spring of Ribs; Pronounced.

Belly; Well tucked up, extending in a curved line from chest.

Loins; Wide and pronounced.

Hips; Broad in proportion to body, breadth of hips being approximately breadth of body at rib spring.

Tail; Docked at approximately second joint, should appear to be the continuation of the spine.

FAULTS: top drawing, too much slope to croup. Long in loin. Soft in back (swayed). Neck, wet, too short and too thick. Not enough body depth (shallow). Thighs lack width. Lacking in rear angulation. Soft in pastern. Too much stop. Roman nose. Bottom drawing, roach-backed. Tail cropped too long. Shoulders too far forward and lacking in skeletal angulation. Feet soft and thin. Hindquarters overangulated. Sickle hocks. Lacking in bone.

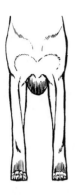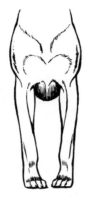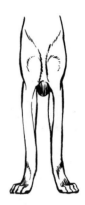

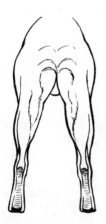

Top row from left to right: good front; faulty in that the Doberman is loaded in shoulder and toes are turned in; narrow, pinched, weak, fiddle front. Lower left, good rear; lower right, cow hocked.

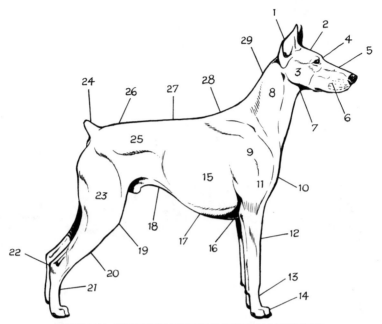

EXTERNAL ANATOMY OF THE DOBERMAN PINSCHER

1, Ears; 2, Forehead (skull); 3, Cheek; 4, Stop; 5, Foreface; 6, Muzzle; 7, Throat; 8, Neck; 9, Shoulder; 10, Fore Chest; 11, Upper Arm (part of shoulder assembly); 12, Fore Leg; 13, Pastern; 14, Front Foot; 15, Chest Cavity and Ribbing; 16, Elbow; 17, Brisket; 18, Belly; 19, Stifle (knee joint); 20, Lower Thigh; 21, Hock; 22, Hock Joint; 23, Thigh; 24, Tail (stern); 25, Loin; 26, Croup; 27, Back; 28, Withers; 29, Crest (of neck).

Forequarters; Shoulder blade and upper arm should meet at an angle of 90°. Relative length of shoulder and upper arm should be as one to one, excess length of upper arm being much less undesirable than excess length of the shoulder blade.

Legs; Seen from the front and side, perfectly straight and parallel to each other from elbow to pastern; muscled and sinewy with round, heavy bone. In normal position and when gaiting, the elbow should lie close to the brisket.

Pasterns; Firm, with an almost perpendicular position to the ground.

Feet; Well arched, compact, and catlike, turning neither in nor out.

Hindquarters; In balance with forequarters. Upper shanks long, wide and well-muscled on both sides of thigh, with clearly defined stifle. While the dog is at rest, hock to heel should be perpendicular to the ground. Upper shanks, lower shanks and hocks should be parallel to each other, and wide enough apart to fit in with a properly built body. The hipbone should fall away from the spinal column at an angle of about 30°. The upper shank should be at right angles to the hip bone. Group well filled out. Cat-feet as on frontlegs, turning neither in nor out.

Gait; The gait should be free, balanced and vigorous, with good reach in the forequarters, and good driving power in the hindquarters. When trotting there should be a strong rear-action drive, with rotary motion of hindquarters. Each rear leg should move in line with the foreleg on the same side. Rear and front legs should be thrown neither in nor out. Back should remain strong, firm, and level.

COAT, COLOR, MARKINGS

Coat; Smooth-haired, short, hard, thick and close-lying. Invisible gray undercoat on neck permitted.

Allowed Colors; Black, brown or blue.

Markings; Rust red, sharply defined, and appearing above each eye, on muzzle, throat and forechest, and on all legs and feet, and below tail. White on chest, not exceeding one-half square inch permissible.

SHOWING YOUR DOG

Are you tempted to show your dog? If you are, be prepared, for with all its pleasures and rewards, it is nonetheless a trial of both dog and master.

Many areas have dog shows for pet owners. Your child can take his pet to the neighborhood pet show, and he will be just as proud of his dog's ribbon as if it had come from the Westminster Dog Show. We can remember the activity in our house when our first dog, of somewhat undistinguished parentage, was made ready for her debut in the school pet show. How she was washed, combed, and brushed! Ginny really bloomed under all the attention, and how proud we all were when she won a ribbon for—being the best-behaved dog in the show. It is good for children to have this responsibility, and also fun to see their pets going through their paces.

But a *bonafide* dog show is another thing again. There are two types of shows—the bench (or unbenched) show and the field trial. Field trials are discussed in Chapter IX, on training. In these shows, dogs are judged on their utility—hunting, retrieving, pulling a sled, etc. It is at the bench show that you see your best bred dogs, vying for the best-in-show reward. These dogs represent the ideal in dogdom—well bred, handsomely groomed, and beautifully behaved. The term *bench show* arises because the dogs are kept on benches (or cages) until they are shown in the ring. Unbenched shows are similar, except that the dogs are not formally benched.

The first show held in America was in Chicago, 1874. Today, the American Kennel Club, which is an association composed of member clubs, some general and some specializing in one breed, sets the standards for the shows. Wherever *bonafide* shows are held, these rules and standards apply.

In general, puppy or adult dogs are first judged within their own breed, sex, age, and group, such as working, sporting, etc. The winners of these groups are then pitted against other winners and best-in-show is chosen. Winners are entitled to a certain number of points towards their championship. To earn the letters "Ch" (champion) a dog must acquire 15 points by wins at various shows. Six of these points must be "majors". A "major" is obtained when a minimum number of dogs in your dog's class (bitch or dog) are entered. The minimum is set by the AKC and differs according to geographical region. It can also be earned if, in the group show, your dog wins, even if his or her class was below the minimum number of entries, *but* others in the group do have a major that day. Your dog is entitled to that dog's points. This does sound rather complicated, and we have two suggestions if you plan to show your dog. Write to the AKC at 221 Park Avenue South, New York, New York for information, or your breed club. Watch the papers for local "match shows". Match shows are not held under AKC rules, but are spon-

Throughout puppyhood, Dobermans must be fed adequately to reach their ultimate show potential.

sored, mainly, to instruct novices (both dogs and owners) in the art of showing a dog. They do not earn your dog points towards his "Ch" but they are invaluable for pointers in showmanship.

The Doberman Pinscher is judged on points for his qualities as follows:

General Conformation and Appearance:

Proportions	8	
Bone-Substance	8	
Temperament, Expression, Nobility	8	
Condition	5	
		— 29

Head:

Shape	6	
Teeth	5	
Eyes	3	
Ears	1	
		— 15

Neck:

Neck:	3	
		— 3

Body:

Backline, Withers, Loins, Tail Placement	8	
Chest, Brisket, Rib Spring, Tuck-up	8	
Shape and Proportions	4	
		— 20

Forequarters:

Shoulders, Upper arms, Legs, Pasterns	5	
Angulation	4	
Paws	2	
		— 11

Hindquarters:

Upper thigh, Stifle, Hocks	5	
Angulation	4	
Paws	2	
		— 11

Gait:

Gait:	6	
		— 6

Coat, Color, Markings:

Coat, Color, Markings:	5	
		— 5
Total		100

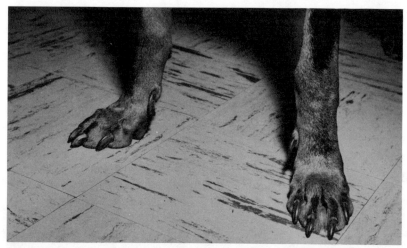

Photograph shows too-flat feet, also bad dewclaws which should have been removed when the puppy was a few days old.

Disqualifications: Shyness, viciousness, jaw overshot more than 3/16 inch; undershot more than $\frac{1}{8}$ of an inch.

Whether or not you intend showing your dog, you can do much to further the Doberman breed by selecting a dog which is up to the AKC standard. If you plan to breed your dog, select his or her mate carefully so that poor qualities are not re-bred and good ones are encouraged.

Are there four of tomorrow's Doberman champions in this whelping box?

Chapter III
Heredity

INTRODUCTION

Once upon a time there was a monk named Gregor Johann Mendel. And this monk had a pea patch. After some time he noticed that he could predict the appearance of his peas. He then began certain cross-breeding experiments and found that he could pre-determine the growth of green peas or yellow peas, wrinkled peas or smooth peas, tall pea plants and short pea plants. From this ordinary pea garden, he produced an extraordinary science—genetics. Mendel experimented with his peas and evolved the early theories of inheritance which so changed the course of biology, agriculture, medicine and other related sciences. Of course, theories of heredity have progressed far beyond anything this simple monk could imagine, but it was his early experiments, unnoticed for many years, which touched off the revolution in the natural sciences.

Each individual is unique unto her, although she will resemble her kind closely.

Animal breeders were quick to use these theories in scientific breeding of purebred stock. Indeed, it is likely that many of them practiced scientific breeding without knowledge of scientific heredity. They bred like-to-like, bred dogs with favorable characteristics to obtain these traits in litters, kept some records of bloodlines for mating purposes. They crossbred different types of dogs to encourage new traits. If they did not know just what it was that transmitted the desired features, they did know that somehow they were passed on to the young.

Good kennel management knows, however, that it is not enough to match up genes and chromosomes. This only transmits the raw material from dog to dog. The environment must also be proper. No matter how beautiful a dog's coat could be, if he isn't groomed and fed properly all his careful breeding will be lost. Therefore, modern breeders take advantage of modern science to breed scientifically, and then take care of the dogs which result from these litters.

THE THEORY OF INHERITANCE

There are many complex factors in inheritance, and modern geneticists are discovering more every day. Many things can influence the dog's breeding—but no outside interference can change his genetic structure, with the exception of accidental mutation.

In every living thing we find two types of cells—soma and germ. The somatic cells make up every part of the organism but one—the germ plasm which contains the germ cells. The germ plasm is the thin thread of our existence. Everything alive, from the lowliest amoeba to the dog and to man himself is dependent for his uniqueness on germ plasm to perpetuate his kind.

Germ plasm in mammals is found in the sperm and eggs of the male and female. This substance contains tiny chemical entities called *genes*. Genes or groups of genes control the form and development of specific physical and mental characteristics. It may take several genes or combinations of genes to produce a certain appearance. For example, any number of genes may control the look of your dog's coat. There are genes to determine color, texture, length, and curliness (or lack of it). All of these factors can act together to produce the black, short-haired, hard-coated Doberman Pinscher.

The geneticist tells us that all the genes are found in every cell of the animal: *in pairs* everywhere but in the germ plasm. Even though

36

Doberman being groomed with a brush to bring out the quality of his coat.

every cell (other than germ plasm) has a specialized function—skin, muscles, heart, eye, etc.—the nucleus still has within it the genetic "fingerprint" of the complete animal.

When the somatic cells are dividing and redividing during the formation of the new animal, they divide so that each gene divides in half. Thus each somatic cell receives the same pair of genes. The germ plasm cells divide differently. They divide to form more cells, but each pair of genes divides in half (one-half the pair), either one gene or the other to each new cell. When the egg and the sperm, each made up of the special germ cells with only half the normal number of genes, unite, the genes again become paired. Each new individual inherits half his genes from each parent, but we cannot tell which half until after he has been born, although we can determine what kinds of characteristics he will inherit from the appearance and genetic make-up of his parents. Since many different combinations are possible, he will inherit characteristics different from those of his brothers and sisters—in fact, each individual is unique unto himself, although he will resemble his species closely.

The important thing to remember is that each characteristic is determined by a pair of genes. How does this work? Why will two black dogs, mated, produce a litter of all black dogs, or litters with brown, tan or blue dogs?

There are two types of genes—dominant and recessive. The dominant is the "stronger", you might say, and whenever it is present it overshadows the recessive or "weaker" gene. You can have a pair consisting of two dominant genes (purebred), two recessive genes (purebred), or a dominant and a recessive gene (hybrid). The recessive gene can show only if both the genes are recessive. But whenever one of the pair is a dominant gene, that characteristic will be the dominant one, although the recessive may show up some time later in another litter.

Let us say that "**B**" represents the dominant black color of the Doberman Pinscher coat color, and that "**b**" represents brown which is recessive in Dobermans. Each dog has two genes for his coat color. Since black is dominant over brown, whenever there is a **B** gene, the dog will be black. If the dog inherits a **B** gene from his father and a **B** gene from his mother he will be black, and will pass only black genes to his children. But if the father with his **BB** genes mates with a bitch with **bb** genetic makeup (a brown color), the children will be black but will be capable of transmitting brown genes. This means that if one of these children mates with a Doberman with a **b** gene, brown *can* appear in *his* children. Simple listings of the combinations possible can enable any dog owner to see all the possible results of successive matings. It is by use of these Mendelian relations that the dog breeders control the quality of their dogs. Practically, it is difficult to see these effects when you only produce a litter or two, but the following variations are possible. These variations become very real when many litters are produced.

1. Two pure blacks mated will produce only pure-bred black dogs: **BB** x **BB** = **BB.**
2. Two purebred browns when mated will produce only brown (recessive) coated dogs: **bb** x **bb** = **bb.**
3. Two hybrids will produce some hybrids and some purebred dogs in the following ratios: **Bb** x **Bb** = **BB, Bb, Bb, bb.** This will show up as three black dogs and one brown dog.
4. A hybrid black and a purebred black will produce some pure-bred and some hybrid dogs, but they will all be black in appearance: **BB** x **Bb** = **BB, Bb, BB, Bb.**

One way of illustrating how the gene theory works is by boxes like the ones below:

Purebred Black (**BB**)
and brown (**bb**)

	b	b
B	**Bb**	**Bb**
B	**Bb**	**Bb**

Hybrids (**Bb**)

	B	b
B	**BB**	**Bb**
b	**bB**	**bb**

Of course, in any single mating these expectations may not be realized, but once you have had many matings and litters you will see the patterns coming up. But since this theory is known, you need not take any chances. You can study the pedigrees and bloodlines of both male and female, and mate dogs which have characteristics you want. If you want brown Dobermans and you know the color is recessive, you must either mate purebred browns (**bb** x **bb**) or hybrids (**Bb** x **Bb**), or hybrid and purebred (**bb** x **Bb**). In the first case you can be sure of the color, the second and third case there is only a chance you will obtain some browns.

Many people speak of a dog's bloodlines as if blood had something to do with inheritance. This is untrue. We should more properly talk of gene lines. Blood itself has nothing to do with inheritance. It is just one physical factor determined by genes.

People also thought that influences on the mother dog while she was pregnant would mark the puppies. We even know of people who think that if the mother listens to music, for example, while pregnant, that the child will have musical ability. Musical ability may run in the family, but this has nothing to do with playing the radio loudly during pregnancy.

MUTATIONS AND ABNORMALITIES

This brings us to the problems of changes in types. There are persons who believe that if they clip the hair of their dog, if the dog is mated, the puppies will have shorter coats. This is utter nonsense, as you can see from the explanation above. The length of a dog's coat is determined by his genetic makeup. Now if the breeder has been striving for shorter coats he can, using scientific methods, mate dogs which through some chance have coats which are shorter than average. Inbreeding and line-breeding will then fix this characteristic, and dogs will be born with shorter coats. In the case of the

Doberman, the early dogs had long wavy coats, but this was deliberately bred out of them.

Occasionally there is a mutation in a breed. Genes are not immune to accident. Changes may come about chemically or from radiation (such as X-rays or nuclear particles), or some mixup in the germ plasm. Sometimes chromosomes cross over and this changes the genetic makeup. These changes are sudden and quite rare. If the breeder wishes to keep one of these mutant changes he can try to duplicate it with inbreeding, but most mutations are downward on the evolutionary scale; only rarely is one an improvement.

WAYS OF BREEDING

Using the knowledge of genetics or the old-time selective breeding, kennels are able to produce puppies which are almost perfect examples of their type. There are several ways of achieving this: inbreeding, line-breeding, out-breeding, or cross-breeding.

Inbreeding: You occasionally hear of "overbred" dogs. People will complain that too much inbreeding causes dogs to be temperamental or spoiled. Inbreeding itself doesn't cause this, but *careless inbreeding* does. Too many breeders are only concerned with how the puppy *looks*, not how he *acts*, so they breed for beauty only. If they ignore the fact that both parents were difficult dogs, overly sensitive, temperamental or nervous (and *tendencies* toward mental characteristics can be inherited), and mate them because they are perfect specimens of their type, you may very well get a litter of overbred, oversensitive dogs.

Inbreeding, by mating dogs in the same immediate family (such as father to daughter, mother to son, or brother to sister) means doubling up on genes. If the father has a black coat and the daughter has a black coat, even if there is some recessive brown, all the dogs will be black and there will be quite a few with **BB** as genetic makeup. Then if you mated the father with one of his granddaughters you would add to the purebred black dogs, possibly getting deeper black. Brother and sister can also be mated very successfully. Of course, if in the course of mating undesirable characteristics show up, you immediately stop mating this particular pair of dogs and their offspring.

Inbreeding among animals is an accepted thing, but is done carefully. Today such inbreeding, or incest, is forbidden among humans in almost every society. In the past, tragic results occurred from inbreeding; for example the European royal families which inherited hemophilia as a result of intermarriage.

Line-Breeding: Line-breeding is mating dogs fairly closely related, keeping within a family, but avoiding very close relations. To establish a strain, dogs must be bred with a combination of inbreeding and line-breeding. *All* modern breeds were inbred and line-bred, if you study their pedigrees.

Out-Breeding: Out-breeding is mating dogs very distantly related, or possibly not related at all, although they must be pedigreed dogs in the same breed for the litter to be registered.

Ten-week-old Doberman puppies. Note that the ears are still uncropped; they should have been cropped two weeks earlier.

Cross-Breeding: The thousands of mongrels you see are the result of cross-breeding, but it is not usually done by breeders at all. However, there are times when it is valuable. In the case of the Doberman, many dog historians believe that the Doberman was part Manchester Black-and-Tan Terrier, and this accounts for his color. They believe that early breeders, desiring this coloration, deliberately bred the Manchester Terrier with the early Doberman Pinscher.

Chapter IV
Inherited Characteristics of the Doberman Pinscher Breed

HOW HEREDITY AFFECTS PHYSICAL CHARACTERISTICS AND BEHAVIOR

Mental Attitudes: Scientists and psychologists are still experimenting with animals to see just how an animal learns. Is a particular trait, such as scenting a trail, learned or inherited? The most we can say now is that certain tendencies run in families, and whether a pair of genes is responsible for this or it is learned through association is not yet clear. Psychologists do know that if they take a family of rats, let us say, which is very good at finding their way through a maze, the children of the family will learn to find their way in the maze more quickly than rats from another less talented family. If you take one of the rats away from its family and put it with another family which is not as adept, it will not learn to get through the maze, but if you put it back with its own family it will learn more quickly than other rats might. Regardless of how a trait is acquired, family characteristics are most important, as dog breeders have discovered through their experience. Many examples are known.

Among all the bird-hunting breeds, the Spaniels are the only ones which are bred to keep their noses close to the ground, hound fashion, when they hunt. Setters and Pointers hunt with heads high. In crosses of Cockers and Setters, the puppies all hunt with heads up, like Setters. Even in crosses of Setters with Bloodhounds the progeny were useless as trailing dogs. When you see a Cocker hunt with head carried high, he probably has some inherited characteristics of English Setter in him.

Some of the smaller breeds are natural tree dogs, and many make squirrel dogs *par excellence*, a use to which only those with shorter coats can be put. Some Poodles tree almost as well as tree hounds

42

This four-month-old Doberman is being stacked to bring out the fine qualities of his breeding.

bred for this. This aptitude is not so well recognized as it should be, although it is by squirrel hunters.

While most persons never give posing much thought, observant breeders tell you how much easier it is to get certain dogs to pose as show dogs than others. There are many who will stand in a show pose when no hand is on or under them. This characteristic seems to run in families.

Gun-shyness also seems to run in families. Many dogs are also thunder-shy. It would appear best not to breed them, although it is possible to train these dogs so that they are not a total loss for hunting or retrieving.

The tendency to piddle is another characteristic which appears to be inherited. Unfortunately, it is often overlooked by breeders. There are too many dogs which panic when strangers or even their masters approach, and then wet. This is certainly most discouraging if your dog is a house dog and you want to preserve your rugs. It can be watched for, and then eliminated, by careful breeding.

All typical retrieving breeds love to retrieve, but there are strains where there is no interest, and retrieving can be trained into these dogs only with great difficulty. On the other hand, you can often see

43

a leashed city-bred dog, familiar only with sparrows and pigeons, get out in a field and display a natural instinct for the art of retrieving. Careful breeding will help to preserve the hunting breeds and keep them from losing these instincts.

Natural retrievers just seem to have to have something to carry around in their mouths. One dog we know came to visit with his master and spent the entire afternoon carrying sticks of wood to the patio. By the end of the day we had a considerable pile of winter firewood, and we promptly invited our friend to come back again soon with his dog to complete the job. Many retrievers will even resort to picking up stools and carrying them around. If you have some old tennis balls around you can discourage this filthy habit.

Some dogs can be taught easily to get the paper or the mail, or even carry something in a bag.

Swimming is also another characteristic that seems to be inherited although the natural tendency has to be encouraged by parent dogs which swim or owners who encourage swimming. Water dog retrievers have to know how to swim, but there is great variation among families and within breeds. If you want to hunt, and own a water-

The finest breeding in the world can be destroyed in a moment by giving your Doberman dangerous material, like these bones, to chew on. Dogs do like to chew, but they should be given chewables made especially for them, with their safety in mind.

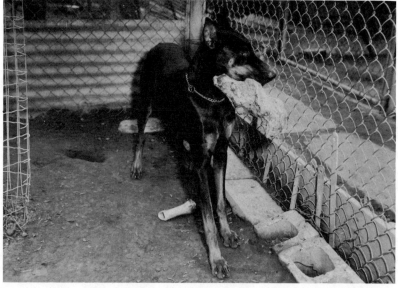

The character of the Doberman is such that he needs exercise. David Miera prepares to take his "King" for a walk.

retrieving dog, or live near water, you will want a dog with this characteristic.

The tendency to contract disease may be inherited. We know that certain tendencies run in human families, such as heart trouble and length of life. Back in the days when vaccines were not available and epidemics were rampant in animal families, it was seen that certain breeds did not have the same early symptoms of distemper as other dogs. Most dogs have convulsions when the temperature first starts to rise, but Cockers and Poodles did not. Although mortality rates were the same, symptoms were not.

Doberman Pinschers are used extensively for police work and guard duty. Obviously, such a dog must have acute hearing, aggressiveness and complete control. He must be easily trained in these areas. It would appear the better part of discretion to mate dogs with these characteristics if they run in families, and to breed out those dogs which shy at gun fire, are poor trackers, or have limited intelligence and cannot learn quickly and reliably. Similarly, where there appears to be viciousness in the family inheritance, this should be bred out as fast as possible.

There is obviously much to be learned in this fascinating field of inheritance. Modern science has expanded and complicated Mendel's simple ideas which he learned in the pea patch, and still has far to go. We can predict the inheritance of physical characteristics such as color, shape, coat, skin, etc., although we cannot always be absolutely sure of the results. With so many factors to consider (such as color, size, coat, etc.), the possible variations are almost infinite in the more complex mammals. As for inheriting or acquiring mental characteristics such as temperament, hunting ability, tendencies for diseases, there is considerable disagreement among animal psychologists, but the consensus appears to be that the tendency to learn these traits is most likely inherited, but the traits themselves must be taught in some fashion.

The Mendelian theories of inheritance tell us how characteristics are passed from parents to children. But, as noted in Chapter III,

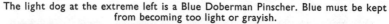

The light dog at the extreme left is a Blue Doberman Pinscher. Blue must be kept from becoming too light or grayish.

the early experiments of Johann Mendel have been elaborated and modified by modern scientists. For more complex organisms, such as dogs, many genetic factors may be responsible for any one characteristic.

COAT COLOR

Theory tells us that we can predict that when two dogs with purebred black coats are mated, all of the resulting litter will have black coats. Similarly, brown-coated dogs mated together will produce only brown dogs. And we can also predict that dogs with hybrid black coats may very well produce both black and brown puppies.

But modern science has discovered also that the inheritance of color is more complicated. Colors occasionally blend or change as a result of the mixing of genes.

The ancient dog was probably a mixture of gray and brown, or derivations of black and yellow. All modern dogs have colorings which were originally possessed by their ancestors, passed down and modified by accidental or deliberate breeding.

The color and markings of the Doberman Pinscher have been carefully bred and maintained. The basic color is the result of the density of color pigments in the skin and hair. The denser the black pigments, the darker the coat color. Less density produces brown, blue or fawn. Of course, genes are responsible for the density. Fawn (or Isabella) colored dogs are not accepted by AKC show standards.

One of the problems of breeding for darker and more richly marked dogs is a condition called *"melanism."* This is a progressive blackening which gradually erases markings or causes them to become muddy and indistinct. The result of this overbreeding can be seen in the Manchester Black-and-Tan Terrier. When it happens to the Doberman, the markings disappear and, as a result, the face takes on a rather unpleasant expression.

The opposite of melanism is a condition caused by less dense pigmentation which often produces fawn or light colored dogs. (The extreme is a complete lack of pigment or *albinism*.)

It would appear that blue coat color is a variation of black, though some breeders believe that it comes from a breakdown of the recessive brown color.

Breeders, therefore, when breeding for more attractive colorings and markings, must aim for certain standards. Dobermans bred for black coats and rich red markings must not be permitted to become too dark and muddied. This is accomplished by occasionally mixing blacks and browns or hybrids instead of always breeding purebred blacks to each other.

Brown dogs are best if the brown remains a medium color with rich markings. There are many shades of brown, but the darker tones tend to obscure the markings and the very light colors may become silvery grays. Blues must be kept from becoming too light or grayish.

One of the problems of breeders is maintaining the rich markings of the Doberman while discouraging any white on the chest. AKC standards allow for only $\frac{1}{2}$ square inch of white. More than that is disallowed in the show ring. Dogs which tend to pass this white down to their offspring are not popular as sires or dams no matter how excellent their other qualities.

Not only do the markings reflect the basic coat color, but also the eyes, lips and nose. The darker the coat, the darker the color of the eyes. Dark brown eyes are the ideal, but browns and blues may have lighter eyes. Very light eyes (hawkeyes) should be bred out.

Similarly, the nose reflects the coat color. Black dogs generally have black noses, brown dogs have brown noses, and the blues have grayish noses. Sometimes a flesh-colored nose or even a butterfly nose (varied pigmentation) appears but this can be eliminated in later breedings. Eyelids, lips and inner ear are also pigmented in close relationship with coat color.

SIZE

The AKC standards specify that male Dobermans must measure between 26 and 28 inches, 27 being the ideal height. Bitches are slightly smaller, 24 to 26 inches, $25\frac{1}{2}$ inches being ideal. A dog's height is measured at the withers.

The size of a dog can determine his usefulness. After all, although a toy dog may sound like 10 dogs if he is yapping loud enough, he is only one very small dog. The medium size of the powerful Doberman makes him ideal as a watchdog. Apartment dwellers are especially grateful for this. He is large enough to be useful, but small enough not to crowd the family.

If these puppies are to attain their maximum size, they must be fed and cared for properly through a balanced diet, timely prophylactic medicine, and protection against parasites.

In use as a working dog his size is also an asset. Many large dogs are not speedy or agile enough to be efficient.

TEMPERAMENT

Animal behaviorists and geneticists are not sure whether certain traits of behavior characteristics are inherited or not, and this is still being investigated. We do know that the best of dogs (from a genetic standpoint) can be ruined by improper training and care. And a relatively unpromising dog can certainly become a faithful and loving pet if he is treated well.

In the case of the Doberman rumors have spread that he is dangerous or temperamental. This probably arises because of his work as a war or police dog. Anyone who has faced one of these dogs doing his job may be inclined to say that the Doberman is aggressive. What he may have failed to note is that the dog is completely under control. He does only what his master orders him to do.

But the ability to patrol a store or a battlefront requires certain traits—a keen sense of smell (for tracking), fearlessness and alertness, devotion to his master. You may not know it, but your Doberman is one of the fastest dogs in the canine world.

49

Although the standard suggests that the male be bigger than the female, this pair can still be considered good and up to standard.

The Doberman appears to be a "born" watchdog. He can be taught to guard a home, protect children and property.

Does this sound like all work and no play for our dog? Not at all. The Doberman loves nothing better than a good romp with his master or the children. In fact he takes a lot of abuse from "his" youngsters. I should add here that children should be taught not to tease or hurt a dog when they are playing. I remember watching in horror as a small child practically pulled the ears off his family dog. The dog let out an occasional whimper and finally ran off, but he didn't so much as growl at his young master (and tormentor). This was certainly the case of a well trained dog and a poorly trained child.

Moreover, a Doberman is generally a peaceful dog. Left alone by other dogs he goes his way. But woe betide the dog who attacks him!

The Doberman is fearless, alert, keen-sensed and an excellent watchdog. In addition he is protective of his master and his master's family and property. All these qualities, with careful training, can be used by families who want a pet or the police or armed services who want a working dog. Fortunately, breeders have recognized this and tend to preserve this as a desirable characteristic. They realize that a handsome dog is a joy to look at, but a dog's character is equally important and they have taken care to preserve the Doberman's unique heritage.

APPEARANCE

The best way to judge a dog's appearance is to compare him with the AKC standard.

In physique the Doberman appears muscular and powerful. But the quality which attracts most people is the Doberman's elegant, proud appearance and handsome coloring. There is almost a noble look as he stands there, compact, sturdy, ears alert, eyes shining.

Early pictures of the Doberman show a dog with a somewhat heavier, coarser look. The coat is thick and wavy, the muzzle coarse. Breeders with foresight must have pictured to themselves the Doberman of today and bred towards that ideal.

As an example, the head of the early Doberman was different from today's, and it is still subject to variation. Time will probably fix the size and shape more surely.

The older Dobermans had head types more resembling the Rottweiler, with heavy jowls and thick skulls. Gradually, the skull became longer so that today's dog can be classified as a long-headed breed. More value is obviously being placed on the shape of the head than in earlier days.

As the length of the head was changed, other parts altered too. A ridge appeared from the middle of the frontal bone to the temples. This was necessary for anchoring the jaw muscles, for as the head elongated, these muscles had to be moved and the ridge became more noticeable. Thus we see both Nature and the breeder co-operating for a better, handsomer animal.

LIFE SPAN

Most dogs live to a ripe old age if given proper care. The Methuselahs of the dog world may even reach 18 or 20 years of age, and 12 or 14 is about average. The Doberman, a naturally robust type, should have many years of useful life, but 13 is a good average.

Chapter V
Reproduction

Would you like to raise a litter of puppies? Even if you purchased your pet with no intention of breeding, there may come a time when you would like to see its offspring. Or, as is often the case, despite all your precautions, someone has gotten into the barn and stolen the horse, and your dog is pregnant, the sire unknown.

Breeding raises many problems for the novice, and we suggest that you familiarize yourself with Chapter III, the principles of heredity, before you undertake to breed your dog for purebred puppies.

If you decide to breed your bitch, make sure that the stud is a purebred Doberman, too. Only in that way are you assured of purebred progeny.

Ch. Damasyn The Solitaire, CDX, owned by Mrs. Bob Adamson. This excellent Doberman is sire of 14 champions, including the first American Grand Victor; Ch. Berman Brier. Sire: Ch. Dictator van Glenhugel. Dam: Ch. Damasyn The Sultry Sister.

Ch. Berman Bangles. Owned by Dorothy M. Maeder, and bred by Bernard Berman, who is shown handling the champion. Sire: Ch. Damasyn The Solitaire, CDX. Dam: Berman Armina.

It is a wise decision for all parties concerned to sign a contract of agreement whenever a female is serviced by a stud. In this way there will be no misunderstandings for anyone.

CONTRACTS

If you are planning a litter of purebreds, your best bet is to go to a professional kennel and arrange for a stud (male dog). Be prepared, however, for making contractual arrangements, and the authors believe that if large amounts of money or complicated arrangements are involved, you should have your lawyer check the contract. In general, there are two types of fees. Most kennels charge a fee for the use of a stud. This may vary from $25 to $200, depending on the dog. If the stud is a famous champion, the cost will be higher. The other type of contract is written so that the owner of the stud gets the pick of the litter. In this case, the breeder has first choice of a puppy or puppies. Be sure that all contingencies are spelled out. In most contracts, if your bitch fails to be impregnated the first time, you can rebreed her with the same dog when she is next in heat for no extra charge. This is called a *return service*.

THE BITCH

A little friend of ours always talks about when his dog is "heating", much to our amusement. But he does understand something about the reproductive process and we feel that this is important. This is an excellent way to explain to children, in as much or as little detail as you wish, the way dogs (and people) are "made." It is certainly far more reliable than the information picked up on street corners from uninformed children.

Dogs, like people, ovulate rhythmically, excepting that where humans ovulate 13 times a year, dogs only come into heat (i.e. ovulate) twice a year. All mammals have the same type of reproductive organs, and although they are not alike in appearance they work in the same manner.

REPRODUCTIVE ORGANS

The female ovaries are located in the abdomen, high behind the ribs. Each ovary is encircled by a capsule with a slit on one side. The capsule is surrounded by spongy tissues known as the *fimbria*. Starting at the slit of each ovary are the *Fallopian tubes*, two tiny tubes which run a zigzag course over each capsule and terminate at the upper end of one of the branches of the Y-shaped *uterus*.

The eggs in the ovaries contain germ plasm, that unique bit of matter which determines your dog's inheritance and assures the continuance of the breed. When the eggs mature, they ripen in blister-like pockets which grow towards the surface of the ovaries. These pockets, called *follicles*, produce a follicular hormone which prepares the uterus. The walls of the pockets are thin and eventually burst, liberating the eggs into the capsule surrounding the ovaries, and they move into the Fallopian tubes and are ready for fertilization. Your dog is "heating."

When copulation occurs (the mating of the bitch with the male dog), sperm are transferred from the male to the female and are moved up the uterus by the same sort of movement (peristalsis) that occurs in the intestines. Within a few minutes of tieing (mating) the sperm are already up in the uterus, through the tubes, and in the capsule surrounding the ovaries.

It takes many sperm to help fertilize one egg; the sperm has an enzyme which breaks down the egg's resistance until one sperm enters. Only one is needed for *fertilization*, and as soon as this sperm has entered the egg, the egg changes and becomes impervious to other sperm.

The eggs, fertilized or not, move down through the Fallopian tubes into the uterus and there, if fertilized, become attached to the uterine lining (endometrium) and grow. Oftentimes, they are not fertilized in the capsule, but meet the sperm in their travels to the uterus and are fertilized and then nest in the uterus. The chromosomes in the egg and the sperm unite, making a complete set. The fertilized egg divides six times, each cell containing the same chromosomes, and at the sixth division one pair of cells are formed which become the germ plasm of the pup. The dividing cells form a hollow globe, which finally pulls in on one side, as if you let the air out of a hollow rubber ball and pushed one side of it in until it touched the other side. If you then squeezed the ball together until you made a canoe-shaped body, and continued squeezing until the two gunwales touched and stayed closed, you would duplicate the process of cell division in the egg.

By the twenty-second day the foetus (unborn puppy) is a very tiny object which is surrounded by protective coverings (the sac) and the placenta which is a band of flesh connecting the foetus with the uterus. At this point, if you put your thumb and fingers on each side of the bitch's belly, you will feel the tiny marble-like lumps which are puppies. These grow and by the twenty-fourth day they are larger and continue to grow until you can't distinguish the individual puppies, as the lumps are so soft. By this time, your dog, however, looks pregnant, as just a glance at her size will tell you.

THE OVULATION CYCLE

As we have already said, ovulation is a rhythmic cycle occurring twice a year, about once every six months. Scientists believe that the changing length of the day is the chief influence inducing the cycle which makes the reproduction possible. As the days grow shorter in late summer and longer in late winter, most bitches come into heat.

This fact can be used to bring the bitch into heat artificially by the use of artificial light. If the length of her day is increased by light, one hour the first week, two the second, three the third, and four the fourth, she can be brought into heat by the end of the fourth week. Even shipping a bitch from one part of the country to the other, where the days have different lengths, can change her cycle. Be careful, therefore, if you move your dog from Maine to Georgia; you may find yourself with a bitch ready for mating.

A more certain method of bringing the bitch into heat artificially is the use of drugs such as stilbestrol, which encourages ovulation.

THE MATURE CYCLE

A female's cycle is made up of four parts; the *proestrum*, the *estrum*, the *anestrum*, and the *metestrum*. She will ovulate during a three-week period and the manner in which this occurs makes it possible for you to quickly get your dog under cover or plan for mating.

The first signs of ovulation, the period of *proestrum*, are an enlarged and swollen vulva and a bloody discharge. The follicles, which hold the eggs, are rupturing, and forming bloody plugs (pits) called blood bodies (*corpora hemorrhagica*) which soon change and secrete a hormone called the *luteal hormone*. The blood bodies become quite tough and are now called *luteal bodies*. This hormone brakes the mating cycle and at this point the dog enters the *estrum* period. Up to now she has not been interested in males. But they are interested in her! She is restless, her appetite may increase and she has the physical symptoms listed above. Now her vulva loses its firmness and within 36 hours becomes flabby and soft. The color of the discharge changes and becomes paler. By the second week your bitch is ready to accept the male and his advances. The eggs are not ready for fertilization before the middle of the acceptance period, however, and since the sperm can only live about three days in the female, you should not mate her before the 10th day after the first signs of discharge, close to ovulation, either a day before or any time during the rest of the period of estrum.

The next two months are called the *anestrum* and the next three the *metestrum*, being the five month period when the bitch is not in heat. After this she's ready to begin again.

If you do not wish to mate your dog, you have only one problem— keeping her from getting pregnant. The careful dog owner will either send his dog to a kennel until ovulation is over, or keep the dog in the house and on a leash when outside. Even so, the male dogs will collect from all corners. It seems that the urine of a dog about

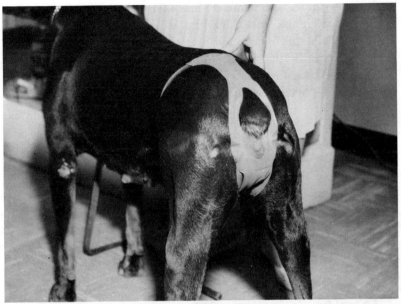

Should you not want your female to be accidentally bred, doggie-britches as worn by this Doberman can be purchased. This belt also protects your rugs.

to come into heat has a peculiar odor which attracts male dogs. Many dogs, when walked on the leash, are taken far from home so that the urine odor is not present around the house. If you live in an apartment, you can purchase a belt in the pet store which will protect your dog and also your rugs.

MATING THE DOBERMAN BITCH

Suppose you have decided to have a litter of purebred pups. When and how should you arrange for this? Your dog matures at about 8 months or more. Some dogs, especially large breeds or toys, ovulate for the first time as late as twelve months or more. Are they ready for breeding? Some breeders say no, that they are not ready, are not mature enough to care for puppies. However, there are many compelling reasons for mating your dog as soon as you can. For one thing, it is easier for a young dog with flexible bones to bear her puppies than an older one. The puppies will be just as good as ones bred later on in life. The bitch can certainly take care of her puppies. Nature provides hormones to aid her. And if she seems awkward with the first litter, this is merely inexperience and she will improve with her next litters. Just think how most new mothers feel about their first child and how awkward each operation like bathing and dressing seems. By the second, things are much easier.

Another excellent reason for early breeding is preserving the blood lines. After all, many accidents can happen to dogs as they grow older and if you have bred your bitch and obtained a litter of puppies,

When breeding some bitches, it will be necessary to muzzle them first.

you have sons and daughters to carry on the "family name." Many professional breeders breed early to ascertain which dogs are the best breeders.

When your dog is ready for breeding, be sure she is in good health. If your bitch is a virgin, you should have an experienced male dog. The virgin may be nervous or jumpy and an equally new stud will only make it worse. The experienced dog knows just what to do and is efficient and calm. Many people send their dog to the kennel and come and collect her when it is all over. But often your presence is required, especially if she is nervous. Generally, your dog is mated two or perhaps three times, once a day, and then sent home. You may have to help. If she refuses to permit copulation you will have to hold her up with your hand under her stomach or, if she is a large dog, with your knee. If she is snappish, a muzzle is required. Once the dogs are "tied," then the stud will be gently turned, and the period of copulation will last from several minutes to over an hour. The reasons for this will be explained later, in the section on the male dog.

After mating it is advised that you keep the female quiet, and she may be serviced again the next day. Obviously, you must be sure that no other dogs get to her after this mating, for if she has not been impregnated the first time, you may end up with a litter of puppies, father unknown. If the mating has taken, you will become the proud owner of a litter of pups about 63 days later.

SPAYING

Suppose that you have a female dog and don't wish to mate her. You may not want to go through the bother and expense of kenneling her when she is in heat or the nuisance of the collection of amorous male dogs outside your door. A bitch can best be spayed before her first heat, at about five months. This is accomplished by a surgical operation called an ovariectomy, when the sexual organs are removed. Many people say that a spayed dog becomes fat and lazy, but this need not be true. If you regulate your dog's diet and see that she gets enough exercise, she will probably remain fairly normal in size.

REPRODUCTION IN THE MALE

Most male dogs can be bred from about the age of a year until they are quite old. Some oldsters of 10 years or more have been known as perfectly fine studs. Handlers feel that a good stud can be mated several times a week for several weeks in succession, but then a rest is in order. Of course, his health must be maintained, the diet good, and condition tip-top. If you own a male and wish to mate him, perhaps for a puppy or two, you will find it more difficult. Most breeders have their own studs and are looking for females. But you may be fortunate to find a breeder or an individual with a female dog he wishes to mate to a dog of your male's characteristics. Again, be sure the contract is properly checked.

REPRODUCTIVE ORGANS

The sperm in the male dog are tiny bodies shaped like polliwogs. They are oval and flattish, with a tail about nine times the size of the body. Each sperm has half the necessary number of chromosomes. But there is one important difference between male sperm and female eggs. The male sperm determines the sex of the puppy. There are two different types of sex chromosomes in the sperm, one the **X** and the other the **Y**. The egg contains only **X** chromosomes. When **X** and **X** unite, the result is a female puppy, when the **X** and the **Y** unite, you have a male puppy.

The sperm are manufactured in the testicles by the germ plasm. The development of the dog's genitals follows a regular course as in other mammals. Before puberty, the testicles, which form inside the body, descend into a loose sac. They are attached to the peritoneum and grow down through the abdominal slits (known as rings) and drop into the sac, which is called the *scrotum*. The testicles are outside the body, as the warmth of the body can interfere with the manufacture of the sperm. But nature sees that they are protected against the weather and other dangers. When it is very cold a muscle pulls the testicles close to the body, and when warm weather comes, the muscle loosens so that the air can cool them.

If a dog's testicles fail to descend the condition is called *cryptorchidism*. Use of the hormone APL, administered by the veterinarian, can correct this condition, but it is considered hereditary and this might make your dog an unpopular stud. If only one testicle descends the condition is called *monorchidism* and the dog with no testicles (and no chance of fatherhood) is called an *anorchid*.

The dog's penis is unusual in that it contains a bone in the front part which aids the dog to achieve copulation. In addition, besides being capable of enlarging with blood, the penis also has an area which enlarges much more than the forepart does. When the male mates with a female dog, his penis swells and the bulbous part becomes at least three times the size of the rest of the penis. This prevents the penis from slipping out during copulation, at which time the dogs are "tied."

When tieing has occured, the semen is pumped in spurts into the vagina. Rhythmic waves which tighten and relax the vagina help also. Some males remain tied five minutes, others an hour or longer. But a five-minute tie can be just as satisfactory.

Introduce prospective breeding partners with restraint, until you are certain that neither party is belligerent.

MATING THE DOBERMAN PINSCHER

If your dog is inexperienced, it is best to mate him when he is about a year old to an experienced female. You may have to push him towards her or even force him. Be sure that the bitch does not snap or bite at him. Occasionally, the dogs may have difficulty mating, especially if they are of different sizes. If you are not experienced, it is best to have the assistance of a knowledgeable handler. He will know all the tricks of the trade and insure a successful mating. The first two or three services are very important and unless they are properly handled, your dog may have trouble mating in the future.

After the first service, the dogs will be rested. If the male is young and not too successful the first time, the handler may let him try again in a few hours. For a new dog, it is best to have a bitch just coming into heat, so that by the time the male is more used to her and experienced, she will not have passed her ovulation period.

Will you injure your dog if you don't mate him? Or will he be oversexed if he is mated often? Most breeders say no. They do feel that it is unwise to start to mate your dog after he is four years old. By this time it is too late to accustom him to the problems of fatherhood. But most unpenned dogs will roam, and will react to the female in heat. If your dog is not kept penned, the chances are that he will find a stray female somewhere. If you wish your dog to be a good stud, it is wise not to let him roam. As you have seen, it is difficult to train the young male to be a good stud. Allow him to mate only with proper dogs, under proper conditions where there is little chance of injury, and he will retain his value as a stud. By keeping a record of your dog's offspring, you will be able to determine in advance what kind of puppies will result from matings with a particular type of bitch. A stud that produces champions is much more valuable than an unproven stud.

Chapter VI
Pregnancy and Motherhood

INTRODUCTION

You are about to have puppies . . . or rather your dog is. The first rule is to RELAX; take some time to talk to your veterinarian about prenatal and whelping care, then sit back and wait 63 days from the day of breeding. Mark on your calendar the expected date—plus or minus a day or two—and prepare yourself. When the expected date rolls around, stay home. One friend of ours left the house in care of a babysitter and came home to find that the sitter had been midwife for 8 puppies—surely above and beyond the call of duty!

PREGNANCY

One of the problems of canine pregnancy is that we sometimes don't know if the dog is pregnant for several weeks after breeding. Rabbit tests for dogs do not exist. Some bitches, even though not pregnant, will exhibit symptoms of pregnancy, which can be misleading and disappointing, if you are hoping for a litter of pups. True pregnancy is unmistakable by around the fifth or sixth week, for the abdomen swells slightly, and the nipples become red and puffy. By the 35th day your veterinarian can eliminate any lingering doubts by a thorough examination. It is at this time he should give you dietary instructions, if any, and other relevant information.

Should your dog be pregnant, both you and the expectant mother will prepare. Nature provides for pregnant mothers by releasing hormones which increase maternal instincts, as well as the hormones which start labor and milk production. But since our dogs are a part of us and we are responsible for their care, we can also help them through this period.

A pregnant bitch requires more food, but should not be overfed. Divide the meals into two, and supplement them with milk and biscuits in the middle of the day. Additional vitamins, A & D, may be advised and 2 to 4 teaspoons given daily is usually the rule depending on the size of the dog. Just before whelping time most dogs cut down on their food. There just isn't room for both the litter and meal. But see that she continues to eat something, especially light meals with meat and milk. You can encourage feeding by giving her favorite foods. In general, dogs thrive on high protein diets during pregnancy and if you have been feeding your dog her usual excellent diet, she should do well.

You must be sure she is exercised, *but* not too violently or under duress. All pregnant dogs should be kept from too much stair climbing and you should try to keep your dog from excited jumping up and down off beds and chairs, or roughhousing with children. One of the problems of pregnancy is constipation, and regular, sensible exercise as well as a good diet will help. You may have to use mineral oil as well to help alleviate this condition.

Some doctors advocate worming around the third or fourth week. It would be best to check with your veterinarian, in any event, because he should prescribe the dosage or, even better, do the worming himself. You can make it easier for the pups to nurse by trimming the hair around the nipples when she is almost ready to whelp. This helps prevent worm infestations and lost puppies.

In days past, before dog became man's best friend, a pregnant bitch, about to whelp, would make a nest. She might scratch a hole in the ground and root around until it was soft and comfortable. But nowadays dogs live in our houses or around them, and we are responsible for a dog's "maternity room." A whelping box is easy to make and maintain. Some people give over the whole matter to the veterinarian and have the whelp at his hospital or a professional kennel with facilities. But most of us want to be near our dog when she whelps and may also want our families to watch. It is a wonderful way to introduce children to the marvels of motherhood, in a wholesome, natural way. You must, however, be sure that the spectators are instructed not to disturb the mother or pups during labor.

The whelping box is a low-sided box which is roomy enough for the mother and puppies. If you have a big dog, be sure it is large enough, at least four feet square with sides one foot high. Your local pet supplier may be able to help you with your selection of a whelping box, but should a supplier be unavailable a homemade box can be constructed of wood with an additional one-inch ledge around the inside, in case your dog is an awkward mother with a tendency to

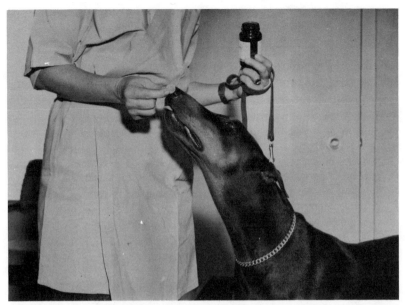

Extra vitamins and calcium for the expectant Doberman are in order. These can be purchased at any good dog counter.

sit on her offspring. One side should be hinged so that you may clean it easily.

Even a large cardboard box will do. Cover the bottom of your box with a piece of linoleum and then a thick wad of newspapers. Do not use rags; they are dangerous and puppies can smother under them.

Where do you put the whelping box? Probably the best place is the warm kitchen, but this may not be large enough or convenient for your family. Some dogs, especially larger ones, are happier in an out-of-way place. Any room which is warm and free from drafts will do. A cellar, unless it is very warm and dry, is not suitable. Besides the physical danger to mother and pups, you will spend your days going up and down stairs to attend to their needs. You want to be where you can see that all those wiggling balls of fur are not getting into trouble, in or out of the box.

Most dogs are used to their own beds or kennels. Be sure that you accustom your dog to her "maternity room," or you may find her whelping in a closet corner among the shoes or out in the garden under a bush.

But most of all, see that you have a peaceful home. You can forgive your dog an occasional upset stomach or indigestion. After all, there's no morning sickness or maternity clothes and the hospital bills are low. Maternity is a natural function of dogs and under happy, peaceful conditions, your dog can be expected to care for herself with little or no problem, requiring only a minimum of sympathetic assistance from you.

WHELPING

You have provided the whelping box, and the mother-to-be has been carefully fed and exercised, and examined by the veterinarian. Now you have your eye on the calendar. Perhaps you have an arrangement to bring your dog to the veterinarian when labor begins, or he is to come to the house. Your dog may start in the middle of the night, when you can't get help easily. Remember, if there is any trouble at all, call your veterinarian, regardless of the hour. A dog, whether she is a valuable show dog or a beloved family pet, deserves professional help if she cannot help herself.

Most dogs, however, bear their young easily. Certain breeds, because of selective breeding, may have had basic body changes, and whelping is difficult. Such difficulty is predictable and your veterinarian's advice will enable you to help the mother over the rough spots. Occasionally, a Caesarian is recommended. Reliable doctors will not suggest an operation unless it is an absolute necessity, because of danger to the mother and the problems of aftercare for the pups.

Be prepared should be our motto. Here is a list of things you can have ready when your dog is about to whelp: the whelping box, lined with newspaper, extra newspaper, towels, cotton, warm water, a scissors to cut the cord, thread to tie the cord, an electric heating pad or hotwater bottles, an eye dropper in case you have to feed the puppies, and if you happen to have them, a pair of scales to weigh the puppies as they are born. It is a good idea, especially if your puppies are pure-bred, to have a pad of paper and pencil to record markings, weight, time of arrival, etc., of each puppy.

How do you know when the event is about to begin? Your dog's behavior will tell you. She will start preparing a "nest," just as if you hadn't provided one for her. All those carefully arranged papers which you put in the whelping box will be torn up and arranged and

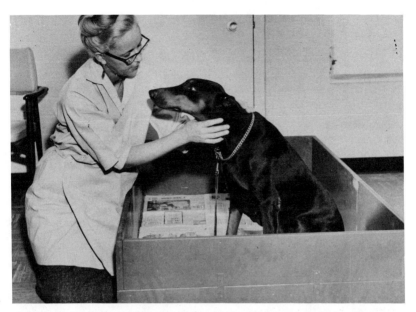

Georgiana Wooldridge introduces her pregnant bitch to the whelping quarters. Note the newspaper on the floor. Soiled papers can easily be removed after the last puppy is born.

rearranged. This is her first maternal act—making a home for her puppies. She will look distracted, restless, anxious, and start to pant. Probably, her last meal will be untouched or she may have some indigestion.

If you have taken her temperature before all these symptoms appear, it will be around normal, 101.5°. About 12 hours before labor begins, it drops radically to 97° or 98°. This is a sure sign. If it shoots up again, better call the doctor . . . something may be wrong!

Real contractions are unmistakable. The dog will tense, hunch up, strain, relax. This is repeated over and over as she settles down to business. The contractions are widening the mouth of the womb and pushing the sac containing the first puppy towards the cervix, which is in the pelvis, now widening to receive this precious package. This is one reason for not allowing older dogs to breed for the first time. The bone and cartilage in the pelvic area harden as the dog grows older and cannot stretch during labor. If true contractions continue more than three or four hours without success, you had better call the veterinarian. This means that there is some problem with the bitch or foetus and delay may mean injury to your dog and the loss of the litter.

If your dog has trouble actually pushing her puppy out, you may be called upon as an assistant obstetrician. The most important things to remember are: *never* put your fingers into the dog's vagina, and *never* force the puppy out, in any way. The best way you can aid your dog is, using a towel, hold onto the sac containing the puppy and gently apply traction to the puppy as it comes out with the contractions. This is only to prevent it from slipping back into the mother. Exert *no* pull at all. Once the puppy is out, a slight tug on the cord will help bring the placenta out too. If it looks as though your dog is having trouble whelping, call the veterinarian.

Whelping takes from 1 to 12 hours but an average litter of 4-5 puppies generally takes about 4 hours. Some take longer. And the puppies can arrive from 5 to 60 minutes apart. In between puppies, take your dog outside to relieve herself or even give her a little milk. But if she is not done whelping she will remain restless and continue straining.

Most puppies come into the world head first, although there are quite a number which make their debut feet first. Sometimes the puppy is preceded by a rush of water as the sac breaks, but more often it is born with the sac intact. The foetus develops in a sac filled with liquid. Each sac is attached to the mother by a band of flesh called the *placenta*. The umbilical cord connects the foetus and the placenta and nourishment from the mother is sent to the puppy through the cord. When the puppy is born, if the sac is still around it, the mother dog, her maternal instincts all working, will tear the sac off, cut the cord, and she will often eat the sac, cord, and placenta which follows it. Nowadays, it seems there are some lazy dogs, and their masters must help them whelp, or perhaps the puppies are arriving at such a rate that she has no time. If your dog cannot aid the puppy, or is too distracted with the next arrival, your help is essential. Break the sac and strip it back over the puppy. Cut the cord about 1-2″ from the navel and, if advised to do so by your veterinarian, tie the cord with a bit of silk string. Some doctors feel that the mother may worry over the string and nibble at it, causing infection. In most cases, there is little or no bleeding through the umbilical cord. The cord dries up and drops off in a few days.

When a puppy emerges, and the mother has stripped off the covering, she will lick and lick it and tumble it about until it is breathing normally, dry, moving and squealing. Sometimes she cannot do this, or the puppy may not start to breathe. Immediately take up the dog in a towel and massage it vigorously. Don't be afraid, you won't injure it. You may even hold it upside down and shake it to clear the lungs. If it still doesn't respond, artificial respiration is next. One method is to breathe into the dog's mouth until the lungs are filled and breathing starts. Or you can hold the dog with the navel away from you, grasp the cord with thumb and pinky and alternately pull the cord and press against his chest with the other three fingers. A third method is to raise and lower the legs rhythmically against the dog's chest. *Don't give up, your chances of success are good.* This often happens when the dog arrives feet first and the cord is pinched or cut before he is out; other pups may arrive this way, so you had better call the veterinarian if you need help.

With a large dog and a large litter, you may want to provide a temporary nursery. A dog in hard labor may throw herself about and her helpless newborn pups can be crushed. Place a box near the mother so she can see her brood, and keep them warm with a hot water bottle wrapped in a towel or an electric heating pad. When you have checked that each little fellow is perking normally, put him in the box. If whelping takes long, and the puppies are crying, you can give them one or two dropperfuls of warm milk—one cup milk mixed with one teaspoon Karo is a good mixture.

But as soon as the mother is relaxed and labor is at an end, be sure to put the pups on her to nurse. The first milk of the mother, called *colostrum*, contains valuable vitamins and minerals and antibodies which give your puppy immunity to diseases while it is nursing. This first nursing also causes contractions in the uterus and helps expel any placental matter or even an unexpected puppy!

When the last puppy has arrived, your bitch is a new dog. She will be relaxed and easy. No more straining, no more anxiety. She will stretch out peacefully and count noses and then put her house to order. You can help by providing new papers and cleaning up.

It may seem impossible, with all that is going on, but you must try to keep count of the number of placentas which come out. There should be one for each puppy. Sometimes, the placenta comes with the puppy, sometimes it follows with the next. But if placenta matter is left inside the dog, it can be very dangerous and your veterinarian should be called. Many dogs eat the placenta, cord and sac. When dogs were wild and not domesticated, this may have served as extra food, but today it is just as well if you remove this material. You are interested in your dog's diet and won't let her starve, we're sure!

Another thing breeders often advise is that you keep a record of the time of arrival of each puppy, his markings and weight, and any other characteristics.

Once in a great while a puppy is born with a deformity. This is very sad, and if the litter is small you will no doubt be quite upset. Harelip is one such congenital deformity, but today it is correctable by surgery. Oftentimes, with harelip, however, the puppy will also have a cleft palate. This prevents it from nursing properly and the dog will starve. Some puppies are born with other malformations, or perhaps the hind feet are turned as a result of the position in the uterus. Your veterinarian will tell you which of these conditions can be corrected and modern veterinary medicine has gone far in perfecting new surgical methods. Discuss your problems with your veterinarian and follow his instructions.

If you have no veterinarian in attendance be on the lookout for the following signs of trouble: labor lasting more than 4-6 hours with no success, excessive straining and pain, trembling and shivering with near exhaustion and collapse, vomiting. Puppies arriving feet first often mean more following in this manner with problems such as tangled and pinched umbilical cords. If any of these symptoms appear, call for help immediately.

We hope that these few problems have not discouraged you from breeding your bitch. Don't worry, most dogs have perfectly normal deliveries and your biggest problem will be to keep from taking the newborn pups away from their mother and cuddling them yourself. We mention problems mostly to help prepare you for any emergency which might arise when you have no professional help at hand.

FALSE PREGNANCY

Once in a great while, a bitch will show signs of pregnancy after being in heat, but will not be pregnant at all. Her abdomen will be swollen, the nipples red and puffy. These symptoms may disappear overnight or she may keep you in suspense until almost time to whelp. If you have any suspicions, consult your doctor. For one thing, if your dog was not impregnated, she may then be entitled

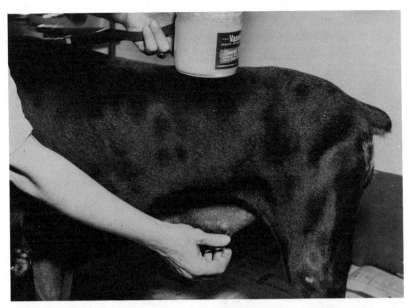
Should the mother's nipples be sore, vaseline can be applied.

to a return service, and your doctor should ascertain that there was no abortion or resorbing of the foetus. Also, false pregnancy is often a sign of illness or malfunctioning in the dog. Sometimes changes are caused by tumors, cysts or infections. If you want your next breeding to be successful, you will have to be sure that your bitch is healthy.

AFTERCARE

The aftercare of your bitch is one of general good health routines. You may have to feed her more often, but be careful not to let her get too fat. Be sure that the diet is properly balanced with lots of protein and milk. If she seems a little constipated (after all, her insides have been severely jolted) a little mineral oil will help.

There is one thing to look out for in your nursing mother. Dogs which produce large amounts of milk or have very large litters often develop a form of convulsion known as *eclampsia* or suckling fits. This seems to be caused by a calcium deficiency caused by loss to the mother during nursing. If this happens, she will start to stagger, lose coordination and suffer from convulsions and often fall

73

unconscious. Call your veterinarian immediately. The most common cure is large doses of calcium given by injection. Plenty of protein after that can keep eclampsia from recurring.

Mastitis is another illness that can plague the dam. This is an infection of the breasts. It causes the milk to become extremely acid and this affects the puppies. It used to be thought that dam's milk had to be alkaline and that any acidity would be injurious to the puppies. This is untrue, as bitch's milk is either neutral or slightly acid naturally. Extreme acidity, however, like any extreme, is dangerous. Using limewater will not cure the condition. The mother dog must be seen by a veterinarian and medicated properly, as soon as possible. The puppies will have to be fed a substitute formula until she is cured, or else weaned altogether.

As for your newborn puppies, more in the next chapter, but there are one or two things to note. For the most part, puppies, like human babies, want to eat and sleep the first week. If they are unhappy about something, they cry.

If one of the puppies seems weaker than the others, put him on the rear nipples. These are bigger and he can get a better hold.

All that young puppies want to do the first week of life is eat and sleep.

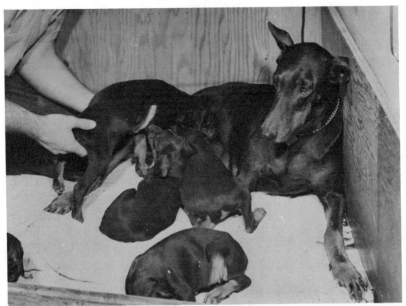

Most females will quickly adopt a puppy from another litter.

You may even have to help him hang on if he has trouble. Another problem which occurs occasionally is when the mother fails to lick her puppy when he is newborn and stimulate elimination. This licking is the only way the puppy can be stimulated to urinate. If she doesn't do this, you are elected. But it's easy enough. Just rub the puppy's tummy and anus with a soft piece of cotton which is dampened with warm water and wait for the puddle. In a few days, he can manage it by himself and you will have plenty of puddles.

Chapter VII
Puppyhood

INTRODUCTION

Have you breathed a sigh of relief? Your dog has come through with flying colors; she has produced a lively, hungry, healthy litter of puppies. Not only that, she is taking care of them with all the love and vigilance a dog can command. Every single puppy is inspected each time it passes review in front of her; each is carefully washed and licked. And she provides her own built-in supply of milk, already bottled and warmed. When she leaves to eat or go outside for a breather, she rushes back afterwards and once again counts noses, just in case she lost one.

Indeed, the mother dog provides all that nature requires: food, warmth, cleanliness and love. When the puppies are old enough, she knows when to wean and how to wean them away from her.

The mother provides all: food, warmth, cleanliness, and love.

A muzzle can be used on a new mother until she learns not to be too rough with her new puppies.

Occasionally, however, problems arise and if so, your veterinarian can help you. Good medical advice and common sense care should prevent any mishaps.

THE NEST

In most cases, the whelping box also serves as the nursery until the puppies are old enough to sleep away from their mother. You may have to add to the sides as the puppies grow so they won't wander away. As long as you keep the papers changed and the box clean, there will be no problem. In addition, the doting mother helps keep the nest clean. She encourages the puppies to urinate and defecate and then cleans up the mess as well. After two or three weeks, however, she may stop, and then you become chambermaid. But take courage, it will soon be spring and then you can take the pups outdoors and your chores will become lighter.

Once in a while, if the mother is ill, or there are just too many demanding little fellows for her to handle, she may neglect to encourage elimination and cleanliness. If this occurs, you can help

77

the puppies to urinate by rubbing their bottoms round and round just like the mother does with her tongue. If they are sore, rub a little vaseline in also. But you may have to clean up afterwards as well!!

If the mother, for some reason, is not in the nest to help warm the puppies, be sure to provide warmth. You can use an electric heating pad made just for this purpose. They are available at your petshop.

DIET

Most dams have an adequate supply of milk which lasts three to four weeks without supplementing. Occasionally, the litter may be so large or the milk so scanty that you have to help out. A foster mother is ideal, but available foster mothers (and willing owners) are hard to find. If you are so fortunate, you will find that it is not hard to accustom the new mother to her new pups. Rub a little of her milk on the puppies' tummies and let her lick it off. In no time at all, they are friends, and if you leave them in a quiet, out-of-the-way place, they will soon be old friends.

But suppose you are not so lucky, and you find that *you* are the substitute mother. It's back to baby bottles and formula for you! If your dog's milk is scanty, you may only have to supplement

A large litter of Dobermans will keep warm by piling up.

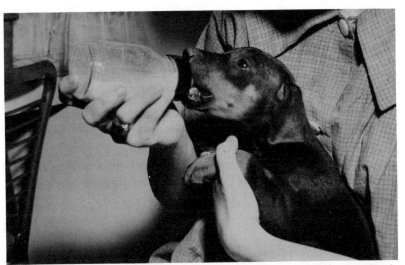

When necessary, a puppy can be fed from a bottle. There are excellent simulated bitch's milk products on the market.

several times a day, but if you are a full-time puppy mother, plan on at least five or six feedings per day. Surprisingly, the care of a young puppy is very similar to that of a young baby, except that puppies grow up faster and you quit walking the floor sooner.

It is most convenient to make up a large amount of formula in advance, refrigerate it, and then pour it into bottles and warm it to body temperature for each feeding. Be sure that the holes in the nipple are large enough and that, while feeding, you are careful that the puppy does not take in too much air (tilt the bottle so that the top and nipple are always full).

There are several excellent brands of simulated bitch's milk on the market. Follow directions, refrigerate and that's all there is. You may want to ask your veterinarian which brand he recommends.

The ideal homemade formula? There are as many as there are veterinarians. If you are making your own, however, remember that cow's milk contains less fat (4%) than bitch's milk (11%). Here are three typical formulas you can try:

(1)	(2)	(3)
1 oz. cream	6 oz. evaporated milk	2 oz. lactogen
1 oz. Nestle's Pelargon	3 oz. water	2 oz. cream (30% butterfat)
6 oz. water	½ tbs. corn syrup	4 oz. water

Refrigerate and warm when needed.

How much do you feed a young puppy? Most dog owners say until his tummy is full and he just lolls back, almost too full to move. You can also tell when he is finished as a little milk will bubble around his mouth. But this doesn't tell you how much formula to prepare. The following chart should help, but remember, these are typical amounts and if your puppies are obviously hungry, feed them some more. If the one you select agrees with the pups, don't change. A change in the diet of a young puppy can be disastrous. This is a good point to remember if you are selling or giving puppies away when they have weaned. Give some of the same type of food you have been giving your puppies to the new owners, or include instructions, so that the puppy's diet does not change.

Weight of puppy in pounds	Amount of formula per feeding in ounces
$\frac{3}{4}$ lb.	1 oz.
1 lb.	$1\frac{3}{4}$ oz.
2 lbs.	2 oz.
3 lbs.	$2\frac{3}{4}$ oz.

If you are only supplementing, you won't have to make up too much, but if you are feeding the puppies completely, better make up a two days' supply at once. Unless the puppies are very tiny, you can probably start them on dish feeding quite soon. If you are having trouble getting a young puppy to drink out of a dish (and after all, what has a dish to offer, it just isn't mother) try dipping its lips into the dish. Instinct will cause him to lick it up and before you know it, that smart fellow will have his mug in the dish and be lapping it up.

The above formulae can also be used when weaning the puppies until you put them on whole milk.

WEANING

Puppies will usually nurse for three to four weeks and then gradually slacken, but you can start weaning them yourself as early as 15 to 16 days, using the proper foods. If left to wean without your help, your mother dog will appear to be doing a most unladylike act— she will regurgitate partially digested food for her pups to eat. She isn't sick; this is just instinctive with dogs. Wild dogs, having no prepared puppy meal or canned and packaged foods, used this as the first food for their helpless puppies, but you can start the puppies

Weigh your puppy at regular intervals to assure yourself that he is progressing normally.

on supplementary foods and relieve your dog of this chore. By now your puppies are much livelier and their eyes are open. They are aware of the world—their mother and their box and those strange people who make cooing noises at them. They may even have tried a little exploring and fallen out of the box once or twice. They wobble a bit, it is true, but they are on their feet, almost.

All this activity and the activity to come mean that the foods you give your dogs now are important. There are excellent preparations on the market for your newly weaned puppy. Use any of the puppy meals; they contain all the necessary nutrients for a rapidly growing pup. Many breeders feel that Pablum or baby cereals are not nutritious enough for such explosive growth, but people do use them with no apparent ill effects. If you use puppy meal or any cereal food, be sure to add milk and fat.

One way of getting a puppy to take to his new diet is to put a little on your finger and let him lick it off. Before you know it, he'll be licking the platter clean. Some people also add scraped beef to a puppy's diet. This is a bother to make, but you may feel it is necessary. Using a spoon or the back of a knife, scrape along the piece of beef

Six-week-old Dobermans eagerly lap up puppy meal mixed into regular milk.

(bottom round is fine) so that what you get is almost liquid beef, beef minus the gristle and connective tissue. Vitamins and mineral supplements are also recommended.

We like to see each puppy with his own dish. This is because the runts (there are often some in the litter) sometimes get pushed aside by the bigger pups; this method gives every puppy his share. Be sure also to have a water dish with fresh water available.

Here is a typical feeding schedule for your weaned puppy.

Age	7 a.m.	Noon	5 p.m.	10 p.m.
4 to 12 weeks	x	x	x	x
3 to 6 months	x	x	x	
6 to 12 months	x		x	
1 year and on			x	

Gradually increase the amount of food you give the dog if he needs it. An active dog requires more food than a dog that is penned up most of the time.

A DOBERMAN PINSCHER PUPPY DIET

Dobermans are large, active dogs and, as puppies, they need lots of bone building foods, meat, milk and fat. The following amounts of food are recommended for your Doberman. Of course, if he wants more or less, make any necessary changes. No dog should be forced to eat more than he wants, or allowed to go very hungry.

Age	7 a.m.	Noon	5 p.m.	10 p.m.
Weaning to 3 months	1 cup puppy meal, warm water, milk	1 cup warm milk with cereal, or biscuits or kibble	$\frac{1}{2}$ cup dog meal, $\frac{1}{4}$ cup meat, 1 tbs. fat	1 cup warm milk with crumbled biscuits
3 to 6 months	2 cups dog food or kibble with water	1 cup milk, biscuits, soft boiled egg 2x a week	1 cup dog meal, $\frac{3}{4}$ lb. meat, scraps, fat	
6 to 12 months	3 cups dog meal or kibble with milk		3 cups dog meal with 1 lb. meat, fat scraps	

Be sure to include fat for a shiny healthy coat.

DEWCLAWS

Dewclaws are small vestigial claws found on the lower legs of some breeds. If your dog is born with dewclaws it is best to trim them off. Because the nails are not worn down as are the other nails on a dog's feet, they can become ingrown and cause infection. Dewclaws can be cut off by the third or fourth day.

WORMING

Chapter XII describes parasites and how they infect dogs. You may be surprised to learn, however, that very young puppies can be infested with parasites, which they pick up from their mother's body, possibly even before they are born. Three-week-old puppies can be wormed with no harmful results. Some breeders worm their litters as a matter of course and don't wait until the parasites put in an appearance. By then it is often too late. Consult with your veterinarian about dosages or let him do it if you are nervous. When worming is done, be sure that your puppies are in good health,

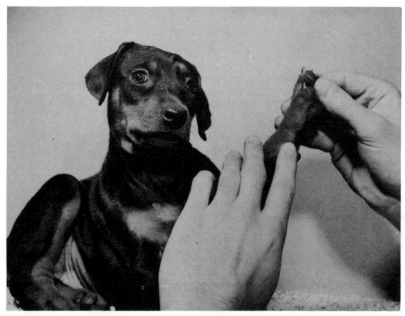

Finger points to where dewclaw has been removed.

or any dose, no matter how safe it is ordinarily, will be harmful. Follow the veterinarian's advice exactly.

TEETH

Puppies, like human babies, are not born with teeth, although there are always exceptions. And like humans, they have two sets of teeth, first or baby teeth and second teeth. The first baby teeth to erupt are the incisors (front teeth). These push out by about 4-5 weeks, and after them come the canines (these are like our eye teeth). The incisors fall out at about 4-5 months and the canines a month or so later. The molars arrive at 5 months, 6 and 7 months. A dog has a full complement of 42 teeth, 20 in the lower jaw and 22 in the upper.

When the teeth are erupting, if the puppy has any illness the enamel will not be deposited on the teeth or the teeth may be pitted or discolored. If the first teeth have not fallen out and the second are arriving, you may have to have the first teeth pulled so that the others will come in straight.

Veterinarians advise that you have your dog's teeth cleaned regularly, as tartar often coats them heavily and then it is difficult to remove.

HERNIA

As your puppy grows, you may see a small lump over the navel. This means that the navel has failed to heal properly and the bulge is a hernia. If the deformity is slight, there is no danger, but if the opening in the abdomen is large enough, a loop of intestine can work out into the sac. You will have to have your veterinarian repair the hernia or strangulation might occur.

SPECIAL CHARACTERISTICS OF THE DOBERMAN PINSCHER PUPPY

Two grooming aids are performed on Doberman puppies. The tail must be docked and the ears are usually cropped.

Docking the tail: In most cases the tail is docked on the fourth day. It does not appear to bother the puppies at all. Your veterinarian

If giving the Doberman a pill is necessary, make sure the tablet is placed as far back on the tongue as possible.

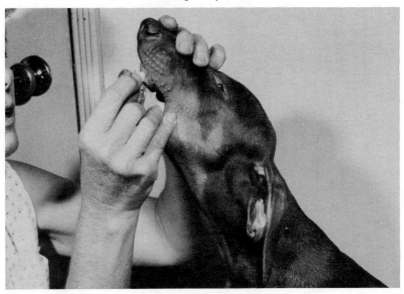

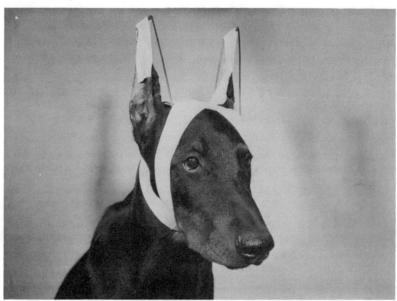

In the process of ear cropping, the ears are taped and racked.

This is how the ears first appear when the tape is removed.

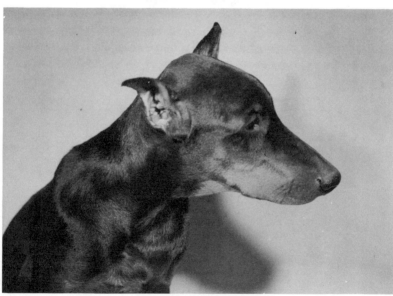

should do it, but if you are forced to do it yourself, it is not too difficult. Using a sterile scissors (boil first), you first pull the skin of the tail back and cut the tail at the first or second joint. Then pull the skin forward, and it will form a flap that heals over the cut.

Cropping ears: Many Doberman Pinschers have their ears cropped, although there are some states and countries where this is illegal. In states where it is not allowed, the AKC regulations do not require cropped ears for Dobermans. The ears are cropped by the eighth week. It must be done by a veterinarian as he will put the dog under anesthesia so that cropping is painless. The ear is cut from the rounded base to the top of the flap of the ear where it is trimmed to a fine point. The ears are protected, often by tape, until healed.

PHYSICAL CHARACTERISTICS

A three-month Doberman Pinscher should look much like his mother or father, only smaller. His coat may be dark brown with deep rust or reddish markings. The body is short and deep with solid straight legs and a shiny flat coat. The tail is straight out and the neck long and arched.

Tails should be docked when the puppy is three or four days old; however, it still can be done at ear-cropping time.

REGISTRATION PAPERS FOR PUREBRED DOGS

There are two steps in registering a purebred dog with the American Kennel Club. First the owner of the litter must send in a litter application with all the details properly filled in. This is sent to the American Kennel Club, 221 Park Avenue South, New York 3, New York. When the dog is purchased, the new owner can apply for an individual certificate, with the dog's name and pedigree. Some breeders have already done this, so that all the new owner must do is have the registration papers transferred to his name.

And, of course, your town may require a dog license, which has nothing to do with pedigree. Be sure and check on the town's regulations for vaccinations, if any, and unleashed dogs.

COMMON DISEASES OF PUPPYHOOD

In Chapter XII diseases are discussed in detail, so this section includes only a few of the common diseases. Be sure to consult the vaccination chart also, as prevention is far more effective than any cure.

Infected Navel: In a small puppy watch out for an infected navel. This is often caused by rough or hard surfaces in the nest. The navel is rubbed and becomes infected. The veterinarian will have to clean it and medicate. The best prevention is to provide a soft bed for your puppies.

Distemper: Distemper is a disease which infects many puppies. It is often fatal or it leaves the puppy with nervous ailments or other serious after effects. Until a puppy is weaned, he is safe, but after that, you must protect him with vaccine. If your puppy becomes feverish, his nose and eyes runny, and his stomach upset, consult your veterinarian immediately. The health of the whole litter is at stake.

Hard Pad: This ailment is most infectious to young puppies. They run a high fever with intestinal upsets. The foot pads are very tender. Call your veterinarian for treatment.

Parasites: We have already mentioned worming, but you can still keep an eye out for parasites such as fleas and ticks. They can infest a puppy at any age. If you keep the nest and other sleeping areas clean, there is less danger.

To prevent injury, carry the Doberman properly. Mrs. Viola Hoskins shows proper method of carrying a puppy.

Deficiency Diseases: To prevent problems such as rickets or other deficiency diseases, be sure that your puppy's food is nourishing and well balanced. Remember that he is growing rapidly and needs more protein in the form of milk and meat, and more fat and vitamins than his elders.

Eye Infections: Once in a while, a tiny puppy's eyes become infected even before they open. The corner of the eye can be lifted up, the eye drained and medicated. See your veterinarian.

Diarrhea: When a puppy has diarrhea it is viewed as a serious condition. It may be caused by a change in the diet, spoiled food, or may be a symptom of a more serious illness. Your veterinarian should be contacted at once.

Chapter VIII
Diet

THE DOBERMAN DIET IN GENERAL

Are you being watched by soulful eyes? Is every bite you eat at dinner followed by your dog, standing there licking his chops, as you put away a steak? And do you give in and slip him just a little bit, or a bone to gnaw on? DON'T, if you want your dog to be healthy as well as polite.

A well-fed, well-trained dog eats, at *his* dinner hour, only what you put in *his* dish. Encouraging dogs to eat food at other times only makes them dinner pests. It may also harm them nutritionally. Bad habits at the dinner table can lead a dog to beg from other people and this is even more dangerous. You know what's in your dinner plate, but unless the ladies have been exchanging recipes over the back fence, you may not know what your neighbor is feeding your dog.

A well-balanced commercial diet is the best for your Doberman.

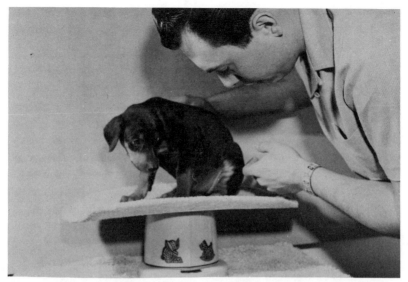
If fed adequately, the puppy will gain weight at a regular pace.

There is, of course, the possibility that you have not been feeding your dog properly and that he is genuinely hungry. Whether he is hungry or just badly trained is for you to discover, but if it is malnutrition, symptoms will appear sooner or later. Surely it is wiser to check your pet's diet and see that it is made up of the essentials every dog needs.

When dogs were not yet domesticated, they ate what they killed, muscle, meat, innards, skin, bones, even the fur or hair. But we don't allow our dogs to forage for their own food any more (nor is there wild game available except in distant wooded areas) and we are responsible for giving them a proper meal. We must replace the ingredients which nature intended them to eat and which were found in the wild game they ate.

THE ELEMENTS OF A GOOD DIET

The essentials of your dog's diet are protein, carbohydrate, fats, vitamins and minerals. Each of these elements should be included in your dog's diet if he is to grow properly, look and feel healthy. Lack of any of the five essentials can cause a number of diseases, most of which are discussed in Chapter XII. Too much of any diet essential can also be harmful, however. People who feed their dogs all the best foods and then give them an extra dose of vitamins or minerals "just for good measure" may cause a toxic reaction in their pets. *Everything good in moderation* is a good motto for a proper diet.

PROTEINS

Proteins are found in meat, fish, some vegetables (such as soy bean) milk and cheese. They are used for essential body building. Meat can be fed your pet if it is fresh, dried or frozen (and thawed). If meat is dried, be sure that it is labeled "Vacuum Packed" as this process preserves the vitamins. Twenty to thirty percent of your dog's meal should be protein. If your dog is pregnant or nursing, she will need extra protein, and so do rapidly growing puppies.

CARBOHYDRATES

Carbohydrates should make up between 50 and 70% of your pet's dinner. They are found in cereals, vegetables, sugar, syrup and honey. Carbohydrates give a dog his boundless energy and help him

Ch. Dictator von Glenhugel. Bred by John F. Cholley. Owners: Peggy and Bob Adamson. Sire: Ch. Blank von der Domstadt. Dam: Ch. Siegerin Ossi v Stahlhelm. Photo by Wm. Brown.

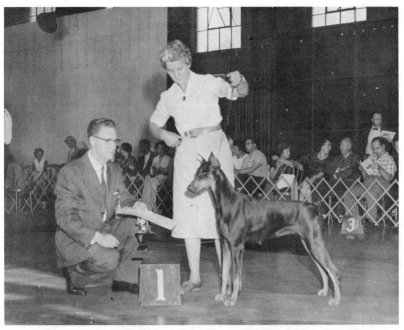

Ch. Fidelia vom Ahrtal. Breeder and owner, Tess Henseler. Sire: Ch. Lakecrest's Thunderstorm. Dam: Ch. Willa v. Ahrtal. Photo by Michael Loconte.

International Ch. Elfreds Curt, CD. Owned and bred by Mrs. Ellen Hoffmann. Photo by Wm. Brown.

Ch. Damasyn The Tassi, CD. Bred by Mrs. Bob Adamson. Owned by Carl Hester. Sire: Ch. Dictator von Glenhugel. Dam: Isolde von Gruenewald.

Damasyn The Easter Bonnet. Breeder and owner, Mrs. Bob Adamson. Sire: Ch. Rancho Dobe's Storm. Dam: Damasyn Sikhandi. This Doberman is the mother of four champions.

grow. When starches are baked, the starches are converted into dextrin which tastes sweet. Most dogs have a sweet tooth and enjoy something sweet and tasty. But if you feed your dog too much carbohydrate, his diet will suffer, as he will eat less protein.

FATS

Fats are also important in a dog's daily ration. Bitch's milk naturally has more fat content than cow's milk, but once a dog is on adult food, he can drink regular milk, and not the enriched formula you fed him as a puppy. You must then add fat to his meal in other ways. This element is important as a vitamin reserve and as an aid for digestion by slowing the passage of food through the animal's intestine. It also keeps his coat healthy and shiny. Fat provides $2\frac{1}{4}$ times as much energy as an equivalent amount of carbohydrate or protein, but you cannot give a dog too much fat, as this may cause diarrhea. Naturally a dog which uses up a tremendous amount of energy, such as a hunting dog, can use more, but for most family dogs too much fat will lead to trouble. Your dog's diet should have about 5% fat content (and not more than 25%) to be nourishing.

Ch. Berman Brier. Owned and bred by Bernard Berman. Sire: Ch. Damasyn The Solitaire, CDX. Dam: Berman Armina. Ch. Berman Brier also holds the German Grand Victor title.

Ch. Axtramiss of Snomis shown handled by Frank Laventhall, and judged by William Kendrick. She was owned and bred by Bernard Berman. Sire: International Ch. Beltane of Tamarack. Dam: Briget of Jun-Har. Photo by Wm. Brown.

Damasyn The Scarlet Scimitar, owned by Ray Kramer. Bred by Bob Adamson. Sire: Ch. Damasyn The Solitaire, CDX. Dam: Damasyn The Little Red Surrey. Photo by Wm. Brown.

Important sources of fats are butter, suet, lard, bacon fat and even vegetable shortening. An excellent and cheap fat is bacon fat or grease from your cooking. Fatty meat is far better than lean cuts, so do not think you are being kind if you buy only the best quality top round steak for your dog; he'll probably look underfed and his coat and skin will suffer.

VITAMINS

Vitamins are those elusive substances without which we would all be undernourished and diseased. They were first discovered by Casimir Funk, a Polish scientist, in 1911. You must see that your dog has a certain amount of vitamins, but remember that if you are feeding your dog a good diet, he will probably get all the vitamins he needs. Pregnant and nursing mothers and pups need supplements, however.

MINERALS

Minerals are also found in many foods and need not be supplemented unless there is a specific need for more. Minerals such as calcium and phosphorus are used to build bones and teeth and are found in milk, vegetables, eggs, soy beans, bone marrow, blood, liver and some cereals (whole grained).

Following is a table of vitamins and minerals, their use in the body and where they are found.

VITAMINS

	Use	*Found in*
A (and carotene)		
Stable at boiling temperatures	General living and growth	Alfalfa-leaf meal
Spoiled if exposed to air	Skin health	Butter, carrots
Stored in body	Fertility, Hearing, Digestion, Vision,	Egg yolks, carotene
Fat soluble	Nerve health,	Fish liver, oil
	Prevention of infection	Glandular organs
	Muscle coordination	Leaves of plants
	Pituitary gland function	Many dark green vegetables
B Complex		
Biotin, Pantothenic Acid	Growth, Appetite, Fertility, Nerve and Heart	Yeast, cereals
Riboflavin, Thiamine	health, Liver and gastro-	Eggs, milk, liver, alfalfa meal
Folic Acid, Niacin	intestinal function	Rapidly growing plants
Pyrodoxin	Lactation, Intestinal	
Water soluble, some destroyed by high heat	absorption	Bacterial growth
Biotin negated by raw egg whites	Muscle function, Blood health, Bladder and kidney function	Cattle paunch and intestinal contents
	Prevention of anemia, black tongue and Vincent's disease	
D		
Irradiated ergosterol	Regulates calcium and phosphorus in blood	Fish liver and oil
Stored by body and can stand heat	Regulates Metabolism	Some animal fats
Resists decomposition	Normal skeletal development and muscular coordination	
Fat soluble	Lactation	
	Prevents rickets	
E		
Tocopherol	Survival of young puppies	Seed germ and germ oils
Stored in body		
Spoils if exposed to air		
Stand ordinary cooking temperatures		
Fat Soluble		
Unsaturated fatty acids	Coat and skin health	Wheat germ oil
		Linseed oil
		Other seed oils

K

Fat soluble Antidote for Warfarin rat poison	Blood clotting	Alfalfa-leaf meal

MINERALS:
Calcium

90% stored in bones	Bones, teeth, blood
	  component
		Bones and bone
		  meal

	Lactation, Fertility	Milk
	Muscle, nerve, heart function	Alfalfa-leaf meal

Phosphorus

Stored in bones, blood, muscles and teeth	Bones, teeth	Cereals, milk

	Carbohydrate and Fat
	  metabolism
		Fish, bones, meat
		  (generally abun-

	Blood component	dant in dogs
	Liquid content of tissues	diet)

Iron

Need in minute amounts	Red blood cells	Egg yolk, liver

Stored in body—65% in
  blood; 30% in liver,
  marrow, spleen; 5%
  in muscle tissue
	Transports oxygen in
	  blood
	Prevents anemia
		Innards, bone
		  marrow
		Meat

Potassium

	Body fluid regulator	Blood
	Blood regulator	Vegetables, potatoes
	Muscle function	

Sodium

Found in body with
  phosphorus, chlorine
  and sulphur
	Regulates body fluids,
	  blood
	Component of gastric
	  juices and urine
		Table salt
		Blood.

Chlorine

	Same as above	

Iodine

Found in thyroid gland	Thyroid health, meta-
	  bolism
		Foods grown in
		  iodine-rich soil
		Fish meal from
		  salt water fish

Magnesium

Needed in tiny amounts	Muscles, bones Nerve and blood function Growth	Bones, vegetables

Copper

Needed in tiny amounts	Forms hemoglobin with
	  iron
		Blood, copper
		  sulphate

Sulphur

Needed in tiny but regular amounts	Body regulation	Meat, egg yolks

Ch. Storm's Donner, owned by Peter Mehlich. From left to right: John Cross Jr., judge; Len Carey, show chairman; Peter Knoop, handler. Storm's Donner was bred by N. Mark Pagano and J. Robert Moore Jr. Photo by Evelyn M. Shafer.

Ch. Brown's Evangeline, CD. Owner, Peggy Adamson; breeder, Eleanor Brown. Sire: Ch. Dictator von Glenhugel. Dam: Ch. Dow's Dame of Kilburn. Photo by Wm. Brown.

English Ch. Precept of Tavey, owned by Mrs. W. M. Cathcarrt. Photo by C. M. Cooke & Son.

CALORIES

Calories are not ingredients of food, but the unit used to measure heat—and food when it is eaten, digested and used can be measured in terms of calories. We are all of us very conscious of weight nowadays. We must not only watch our own figures but our dog's as well. Dogs can eat 30 to 50 percent more food than they need and still be hungry. Very small dogs, between 5 and 10 pounds, need 250 to 600 calories daily. Dogs weighing between 15 and 25 pounds use at least 600 to 1,000 calories and dogs from 30 to 60 pounds use up 1,100 to 2,000 calories. If your dog is eating more than he should, you may have to put him on a diet, or hope for a dog-type food substitute.

COMMON TYPES OF DIETS

You now know the elements of a proper diet for your dog, but you may be wondering how to apply all this knowledge to what to put into your dog's dinner plate. There are a number of different types of diets available. Your pocketbook and the type of household you have will determine what kind of food you feed your dog. Your dog's size will dictate how much food you must provide. Certain types of hounds are deliberately kept thin, but most dogs look and feel best when their bodies are filled out, their coats glossy and the skin healthy. This is achieved with a proper diet. Remember that puppies will eat much more than adult dogs in terms of their weight, and that active dogs will consume more than their less active canine brothers.

TABLE SCRAPS—OR HOME DIETS

Nowadays, with modern methods of refrigeration and freezing, there is very little left over after meal times. Most food is consumed, and the scraps often used by the thrifty housewife to concoct the latest casserole the next day. Thus, it would appear that in order to feed your dog properly from table scraps, you have to purchase more food than you eat. Spoiled food, of course, is for the garbage can, not the feeding dish. The only leftover that you can give him easily and cheaply is surplus grease and gravies.

A homemade dinner for your pet can be made up as follows: ground fatty beef or liver, innards or even cottage cheese to provide protein, some green or yellow vegetables, a cereal such as oatmeal or day-old whole wheat bread spread with butter and crumbled up,

Doberman receives instructions that table scraps are not for him.

milk or warm water, a cooked egg several times a week, even cooked fruit, and of course leftover gravies, fat and scraps. Of course, this can cost you from 50c. to $3 per day per dog!

CANNED DOG FOOD

Canned dog food is very cheap and very easy to prepare—a can opener is all you need. But be sure if you use this as the staple diet of your dog, that you know the true cost of the food and the protein content. Most canned dog food contains 70-75% water and the remaining 25% is food. A good-sized dog will need at least 2-3 cans of dog food a day, if it is not supplemented with other foods, regardless of what the label tells you. Another thing to watch out for is the quality of the canned food, although this may be difficult to discover. It is sad, but true, that many canned dog foods are not high quality and that the meat is of such low quality that you would never knowingly feed it to your pet. There are some good quality products, of course, put up by companies genuinely concerned with your dog's health and well being. Compare the protein and fat guarantees printed on the label. The more of each, the better the food. Or ask your veterinarian to recommend a good canned dog

Ch. Votan v Gruenewald II. Bred by Earl Spicer, and owned by Willie Deckert. Sire: Ch. Dictator von Glenhugel. Dam: Ch. Hanschen v Gruenewald.

An easy way to blend a formula for small puppies.

food and check the label for content. The Dept. of Agriculture issues a seal of approval for canned dog food which meets minimum nutritional standards.

KIBBLES WITH MEAT AND VEGETABLES

Kibbles are a form of biscuit but they are by no means a complete diet. Flour is the chief ingredient and as it is baked it is converted into dextrin which tastes sugary. Dogs love it and lick their lips for more. But the baking process destroys the vitamin and mineral content while it increases its dog appeal. Therefore you must add meat, vegetables and, often, vitamin and mineral supplements. You may find it is a nuisance to mix. If kibbles are used with no other added foods, this menu can cause serious diet deficiency diseases and even convulsions.

PELLETS

A number of commercial dried dog foods are available in pellet form. They can be eaten dry or with a little water, and extra water served on the side. Their chief attraction seems to be that they are easy to pour and "look nice."

Chuck Latter mixes vitamin and mineral supplements into kibbles to be fed to a crowd of Dobermans.

MEALS (OR DRY DOG FOOD)

By far the most popular food in kennels is dog meal. It is also the most versatile of the packaged dog foods. All the essential vitamins and minerals are added in sufficient quantities, as well as protein. Some brands carry as much as 30% protein. If you use 1½ ounces of fat to 5 ounces of high quality meal, you have a dinner that cannot be surpassed for quality, nourishment and dog satisfaction. As an added inducement, it is easy to prepare, and extremely economical. Pregnant and nursing mothers will need extra milk and meat with their regular dinner. Special puppy meals are also available for growing dogs.

EXTRUDED FOODS

Extruded foods are a fairly new product made in the same way as puffed wheat or rice. The granules of starch are heated under great pressure and when the pressure is suddenly released, the granules explode—they are shot from guns as the ads say! Of course, this food tastes sweet and is enthusiastically greeted by dogs and you may

Ch. Hagen v. Ahrtal. Bred and owned by Tess Henseler. Sire: Ch. Delegate v.d. Elbe. Dam: Meadowmist Isis of Ahrtal. Photo by Wm. Brown.

Ch. El Campeon's Gallito, bred by Mr. and Mrs. Robert White, and owned by Linda K. Blessing. From left to right, Dr. D. Davidson, judge; Johnny Davis, handler; Linda Blessing, owner. Photo by Norton of Kent.

think that this is an ideal food. But this eagerness may be hunger—real hunger. The food is blown up to twice its original size, and therefore the animal eats only one half his usual ration and he is full. But he is only getting one half his needs. The results are hunger and undernourishment, surely a poor investment for your pet.

DIET COST

Following is a table showing the various diets and their relative cost, based on feeding a 25-pound dog 900 calories a day. The prices may vary somewhat, depending on where you live.

Type of Diet	Cost per day	Cost per year
1. Canned dog food (2 for 29c.)	.29	105.85
2. Kibbles, meat, vegetables, supplement vitamins—18c. per lb., others app. vitamin supp. 5c. per day)	.38	138.70
3. Pellets 15c. per pound	.084	30.66

Efficiency is the key word at this large Doberman Pinscher kennel, especially at feeding time.

4.   Dry dog food plus fat (14c. per pound for meal, fat free from your table)   .04   14.60

The above list shows that the last type of diet is by far the most economical. The authors suggest that when you are planning your first trip to the market or pet store for supplies for your new pet, that you take this book along or a list of the necessary elements for a good diet. Check the contents of each type of dog food and the cost.

Once you find a good nutritious diet for your dog, stick to it, as changes can cause intestinal upsets, especially in puppies. Of course, if your dog is hardy and has a good digestion, you may find yourself adding leftovers to his basic diet, especially those he loves. But be sure that these tidbits do not take the place of the really important proteins, vitamins and minerals. For a treat, you can give your dog biscuits or dog treats. A friend with a large, active, almost grown dog finds that biscuits are a fine substitute for furniture. Whenever she finds that her dog is about to test the durability of the sofa, she gives him a handful of dog treats and this satisfies him.

QUANTITY

Just how much do you give a dog? Breeders recommend that you plan on $\frac{1}{2}$ to 1 ounce of food per pound of body weight, depending

Ch. Bailes Apache of Gracewood, owned and bred by Mrs. Boyce Bailes. Left, Ed Bracey (handler), and Robert A. Moseley (right), judge. Photo by Alexander.

on the amount of exercise and the age of the dog. Feed your dog once or, in winter, twice a day. Oftentimes, in winter, dogs appreciate a light breakfast in order to help them face the school bus, mailman, garbage man and other sundry daytime activities. The main meal, however, should be given in late afternoon or early evening.

WATER

Have water available at all times. If you do not wish to keep the water dish out, offer water at least three times a day. You may want to restrict water to a puppy just before night, or in the case of illness.

DISHES

The best type of dishes are aluminum, but you can also purchase plastic or ceramic feeding pans. They do not chip or break easily, and can be cleaned quickly. Be sure that feeding and water pans are clean at all times. When you set out your dog's dinner, allow him at least 20-30 minutes to eat it, but then take it away and do not feed your dog until his next regularly scheduled meal time. This keeps him from being finicky and picky about his food. Naturally, if he is

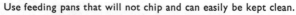
Use feeding pans that will not chip and can easily be kept clean.

Damasyn The Waltzing Raven, bred and owned by Joseph Rapisarda, is the dam of four champions. Sire: Ch. Damasyn The Solitaire, CDX. Dam: Damasyn The Winterwaltz. Photo by Wm. Brown.

ill or has some diet problems, you will have to adjust. Another hint is to be sure that the food is not too sloppy and watery, so it's not messy.

Put your dog's dish in the same place at every feeding, preferably a spot where he won't be disturbed.

A TYPICAL DOBERMAN PINSCHER DIET

Doberman Pinschers of one year and over are large, active dogs. They need plenty of food to give them energy. Feed your dog twice a day if necessary. For a normal-sized dog plan on between 4 and 5 cups of meal a day plus 1 pound of meat. You can use water or milk to moisten it, add a coddled egg occasionally, and of course, fat.

SPECIAL FEEDING PROBLEMS

Pregnant Bitches: Pregnant bitches need extra food, especially meat and milk, as well as extra vitamins. Feed your dog as much as she wants, but make sure that she doesn't get overweight. Toward the end of her pregnancy, keep the meals light.

Nursing mothers: Lactating bitches also need extra food, with meat, milk and vitamins especially essential. You may find it better to give her several meals a day so her milk will be rich.

Weaning: The chapter on puppyhood (Chapter VII) discusses puppy diet. The main thing to remember is that bitch's milk is richer than cow's milk and that when the puppies are weaned, you will have to add fat to the milk you feed them. You must also plan that puppies eat much more than adult dogs of the same size. Once they grow up their food intake will stabilize, but while they are growing, be sure to feed them highly nutritious foods and rich milk. There are several excellent puppy foods which can be mixed with milk and used for puppies.

Puppies must learn to eat meat and solids when being weaned.

Ch. Barlynn's Clean Sweep, bred by Pete Knoop and owned by Mrs. Ellen Hoffmann. Sire: Ch. Delegate v.d. Elbe. Dam: Kitchawan's Emma v. Grunberg. Also pictured are Mrs. Ruth Castellano (left), judge, and Mrs. Ellen Hoffmann, handler. Photo by Wm. Brown.

Reducing: Overweight is a national concern. Everyone is on a diet, it seems, and diet foods and fads are a billion dollar business in this country. Your dog may not be conscious of his or her figure, but you should be aware of it. Fat dogs are prone to illness and unfit for showing. But dieting is heartrending. After all your dog doesn't know what it is all about and he can't rejoice in every lost pound on the scale. You MUST resist his appeals for more food, and tell your children (sternly) not to feed him, also.

To help a dog reduce, cut his caloric intake down so that he must live on his stored fat. If your dog normally eats 900 calories, then cut him down to 500. One cup of dog meal plus water should be enough. In ten days he will have lost about 1 pound. Exercise is also helpful. Check with your veterinarian for a proper diet for your pet if he is overweight.

Ch. Juno vom Ahrtal, owned and bred by Tess Henseler. Sire: Ch. Fortuna's Maestro. Dam: Ch. Zessica v. Ahrtal.

Ch. Zessica v. Ahrtal, owned and bred by Tess Henseler. Sire: Alaric v. Ahrtal, CDX, TD. Dam: Ch. Friederun v. Ahrtal. Photo by Wm. Brown.

Chapter IX
Training

PRINCIPLES OF TRAINING YOUR DOBERMAN

In today's world of fast-moving cars and crowded cities and suburbs, the life of a dog is truly a *dog's life* if he is improperly trained. The many hazards of living mean the survival of the fittest—and to be fit for today's world a dog must be properly trained to obey his master (or mistress).

The methods are standard with dog trainers—positive training which relies on encouragement and reward, either by praise from the trainer or food, and negative training where mistakes are punished. Combinations of these methods are common.

With either reward or punishment, animal training requires that each step be taught slowly and completely before the next step is introduced. Rewards (positive training) can be *praise* by tone of voice and petting, or *food* such as a favorite tidbit, dog candy or biscuits.

The authors believe that the best and most enduring type of training is positive training, using only the master's voice in praise. Dogs trained with candy or other foods come to rely on this rather than on the person making the command. Of course, this does not mean that you should not occasionally reward your obedient dog with a bit of his favorite food. In extreme cases, you may have to use punitive measures once in a while to convince him of the error of his ways, but this should not be the standard training method for your dog.

Dogs trained negatively with punishment—and some trainers advocate switches or chains thrown near the dogs, paper, or hitting—may become vicious. By and large, most dogs respond to violence in kind. Dogs are not born vicious; they are made so. The uncontrollable dog could have been saved by thoughtful training work when he was young or less wild. Sadly, in most cases, the dog who is mean or wild has to be destroyed, or is killed as a result of his foolhardy actions.

There are two types of training your dog can have—*general training* which makes it possible for him to live with the family in peace, and *specialized training* to qualify for the AKC Obedience Trials. Of course, you can also teach your dogs many tricks such as playing dead or begging, for your own enjoyment. Hunting dogs, police and army dogs, and other working breeds need special training. It is most often taught by experts in the field rather than by lay persons.

When you begin training remember the following: your puppy is anxious to obey you, and is really trying hard even if he doesn't quite succeed at first. Every ounce of puppy love wants to please you. If he can't quite make it the first time, be PATIENT. He will make the grade in time when his muscles are all working properly and he has mastered the first steps. Be CONSISTENT. Use the same word for the same command, and react the same way to his success or lack of success. Don't laugh at something he does one time and then punish him for it the next. Use your VOICE, not your hand, to punish. Very little can be accomplished by beating a dog except to frighten him.

When a dog has done something that you wanted him to do, take time out to praise him. He'll train quicker that way.

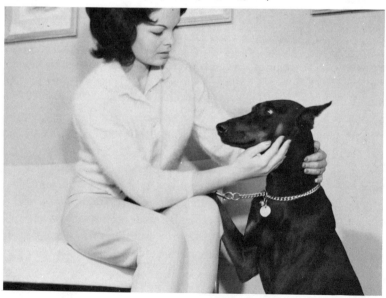

Tri-International Ch. Borong The Warlock, CD. Bred and owned by Henry and Theodosia Frampton. Photo by Evelyn M. Shafer.

Teach your dog ONE STEP AT A TIME. He can't learn the more complicated actions until he has mastered the elementary ones. REWARD your dog immediately if he does it right. Although you can use a treat, we believe that by complimenting your dog and showing him with your voice and mannerisms what a wonderful dog he is, how marvelously well he has learned to sit and how pleased everyone is with him, that he will answer with just oodles of love and willingness to learn more. PUNISH your dog if he refuses or disregards your commands by speaking angrily to him and making him realize that you are displeased; do not use violence or withhold basic necessities such as food.

HOUSEBREAKING

Do you have a new puppy? Or has one of the litter remained behind? The very first training you will have to start is *housebreaking*. This is imperative if everyone is to live together harmoniously and in clean quarters. But puppies, like children, cannot be completely trained until they are more mature physically. When you hear of a toilet trained child of nine months, you can be sure that his mother is trained, not the baby. And so it is with dogs. Most dogs cannot be

117

completely and reliably housebroken until four months of age, when their bladder and anus are under control. This is no cause for despair, however; there is plenty you can do until then to keep the house and your dog's quarters clean.

Most dogs are first paper-broken, unless they live outdoors. A dog will not deliberately mess his bed, but he will look around for a convenient corner. The first thing you must do with a young puppy is to confine him to a fairly small space and cover that space with newspaper. Then he can mess to his heart's content.

If you allow your puppy freedom of the house, you are asking for trouble. But if he does get out and make a puddle right in the middle of the floor, be sure to wipe it up thoroughly. Use a special dog scent to remove the odor, or your dog will make a beeline for that spot the minute he escapes again. Once he is trained, you can gradually allow him the run of the house, but keep an eye on him for danger signs.

Dogs instinctively use the same place over and over again. Observe which corner he calls his own, and gradually begin removing the paper until only that spot is covered. Leave a bit of soiled paper

Ch. Bailes Tessa The Tempest, owned and bred by Mrs. Boyce Bailes. Here she is being shown handled by Joe Gregory (left), with judge Henry H. Stoecker holding her newly won ribbon. Photo by Wm. Brown.

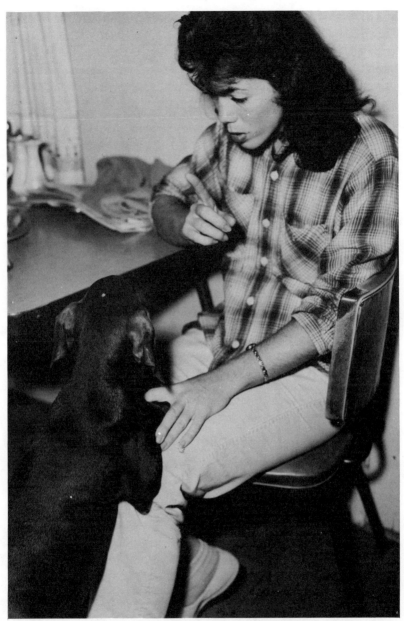

If you don't want your Doberman to come near the table, train him as a puppy not to. As in all training, be consistent. Do not permit him to do something one day and not the next.

there so that the odor will attract him back. Praise him lavishly if he continues to use the spot. Be sure he knows that you are terribly pleased that he has been such a good dog. Of course, he probably won't know what it's all about for a while, but that's all right; he loves it anyway. Dog scents are available at most petshops to aid you in training your dog should you prefer a more sanitary training method.

As your dog grows up a bit, you will notice that he has to eliminate less and less. Mostly he goes right after naps, meals or play. Now is the time to start housebreaking. Those people who live in apartments have a more difficult job. They must note the signs, pick up the dog, rush to the elevator and race outside to the nearest curb, trying to attach the leash and desperately hoping the dog won't wet in some embarrassing place like the elevator. If you live in a house or garden apartment, your job is considerably easier. As soon as you observe the dog beginning to sniff around or go in circles, grab him and head for the outdoors. Be sure to praise and pat him generously when he cooperates. If you lead him to the same spot each day, the odor will remind him of his job. It's amazing how quickly your dog will learn what all these mad dashes outside mean and obey you willingly. Besides, he generally has to go! This does make it easier. There will be lapses occasionally. If your dog wets the rug or messes the kitchen floor, immediately chastise him with your voice. Let him know how

Right after a meal is a good time to introduce your Doberman puppy to the paper he is to use.

If he does his job on the paper, praise him. Don't punish him if he doesn't get the idea right away.

ashamed you are and how disgusted you feel. Never hit him, never rub his nose in his own mess, and never wait an hour or so before punishment. Dogs have short memories when they are young, and even 15 minutes later he won't have the least idea what you are talking about. If the lapse is just temporary, you are in luck. Occasionally you may have to begin again. This sounds discouraging, but it is the only way to housebreak him properly.

The following hints may be helpful:

1. **Remember that your small puppy has to go quite frequently, and you should be prepared to take him out. You must plan to be home while this basic training is completed.**
2. **Remember to take him out after naps, meals, play, or any excitement (such as strangers in the house or other dogs).**
3. **Praise your dog when he cooperates. Use your voice only when he forgets. And don't expect him to learn the day you begin. Training takes time and the dog must be physically mature.**
4. **If you let your puppy roam the house, you are asking for trouble; keep him confined to one room until you are absolutely sure.**

Ch. Felix vom Ahrtal, bred and owned by Tess Henseler, also shown handling the champ. Judge (left) is Carl Seishab. Sire: Ch. Lakecrest's Thunderstorm. Dam: Ch. Willa v. Ahrtal.

Ch. Taina vom Ahrtal, bred and handled in the photo by Tess Henseler. Owner is Evelyn L. Ahr. Judge (left) is Chris Shuttleworth. Sire: Ch. Felix vom Ahrtal. Dam: Iduna vom Ahrtal. Photo by Wm. Brown.

Damasyn The Waltzing Raven, bred and owned by Joseph Rapisarda. Sire: Ch. Damasyn The Solitaire, CDX. Dam: Damasyn The Winterwaltz. Photo by Wm. Brown.

EARLY TRAINING

COME: This should be the first actual training you give your dog aside from housebreaking, and it is the most important. Once your dog learns to **come** when you call, he is safe from many dangers, and more easily handled.

A puppy should not be forced, so the easiest way to begin training him to **come** is to begin while is he in the house. Just coax him to you, saying **come** in your most wheedling voice. If there is no other big attraction—such as dinner or strangers—who should he come to but you, who else is so willing to play and means warm food and affection? He will sidle up at the sound of your voice, just begging for a pat. And of course you give him one. Repeat this several times a day, using only the one word **come.** Do not keep the lesson up for long and don't punish if he does not obey. Try again, perhaps with a bit of food. When he obeys fairly well, try it outside. Select a quiet spot and call **come.** If he refuses to come to you, take courage in hand and run off. You may fear you will lose him but no puppy can refuse a good chase with his master. If you look around you will see him manfully trying to catch up with you. When he does come up, praise him, pet him, make a big fuss, don't scold him for not obeying immediately.

Once your dog has begun to catch on to the new word in his vocabulary, you can begin adding his name, so he gets used to that. **Come, Kippy** and then **Kippy, come** will teach him his rightful name.

NO and **STOP:** About the same time as you begin teaching your puppy to come to you, you will probably find yourself telling him **no** or **stop.** He's in and out of mischief, and you are spending your days trailing him around to see that he isn't puddling as well as keeping him from chewing up the furniture and turning over the garbage can. If he does get into something he shouldn't, shout a loud **no** or **stop** and then take him away firmly. If he's bent on chewing, give him a rawhide bone and confine him to his room. But be sure and practice consistency. What is forbidden one time should

Ch. Majakens Bronze Erick, bred and owned by James G. Kennedy. From left to right: Marlene Kennedy (handler), Mr. Adaire (judge). Photo by Wm. Brown.

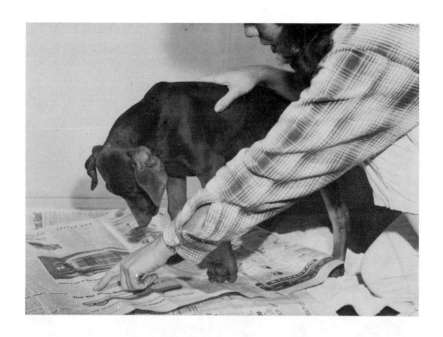

As your Doberman grows older, he will soon understand the purpose of the paper. After he has done his job, lavish praise on him. Before long your pet will be house-broken.

A choke collar and leash are excellent tools for training a dog.

If you don't want your Doberman to sit on furniture as an adult, don't permit him to do so as a pup.

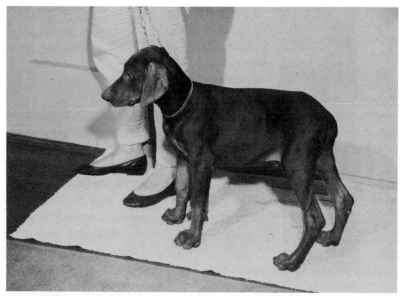

When you are walking a Doberman on a leash, the dog should be on your left side.

also be forbidden the next, or you may find yourself with a very confused puppy. As a rule it isn't enough just to say **no,** but you must also remove him from the temptation or take the temptation away from him.

Stop can be used when you want the puppy to stop some activity such as biting, barking and growling. Often you will have to close his mouth and hold it shut while you chastise him with **stop** and a most sorrowful look.

LEAD TRAINING

Your dog is housebroken and almost knows when to **come,** and you can begin to think about lead (leash) training. Again, you must have time for training. If you have no spare time, perhaps it would be better to arrange for a professional trainer or school. If you plan to do it yourself, then be prepared to allot sufficient time.

The best type of training collar is a choke collar. This is a collar made of chain, with a ring where the lead is fastened. Slip the collar over the dog's head and attach the chain. A choke collar pulls tighter when you do, and loosens when you let up. It should be removed when not in use.

Use a sturdy collar so that it does not harm the dog. The lead can be of leather or chain. Be sure it is strong enough if you have an energetic puppy. When you attach the lead to the collar, have it pass over the dog's neck, not under it.

Suppose you collar your dog, attach the lead, and set out for a pleasant walk with him. The first thing he does is refuse to move. Or perhaps he moves too much, rushing off, and bounding in all directions until brought up by the lead. What now? Obviously, you and this whirling dervish cannot go parading down the street. In the first place, see that you are holding the lead and dog properly. The dog should be on your left side, the lead held in the right hand with your left hand available for extra strength and guidance. If your dog refuses to go with you on a leash, take him home. Let him get very hungry, then attach the leash and lead him to his food. If he associates good things with the collar and lead, he will be more cooperative the next time you plan an outing.

HEEL: What happens if he rushes off, pulling you along? We have seen any number of people being dragged along by their dogs, and this is surely a sign of poor training. If your puppy runs off, jerk the

Ch. Damasyn The Flame, bred by Bob Adamson and E. Prziborowski. Owned by Eldon R. Prziborowski. Sire: Ch. Dictator von Glenhugel. Dam: Damasyn The Flaming Sable.

Ch. Agitator of Doberland, bred and owned by Ivan Wolff. Sire: Dictator von Glen-hugel. Dam: Pinsch of Doberland.

lead with the left hand and then stop, say **come,** and wait for his return. Praise him when he comes back. Sooner or later your dog will see that his wildness only results in stopping the walk altogether and general disapproval. Don't pull, incidentally, just jerk firmly but not unkindly. If you are full of admiration when he does come back, he will do it more willingly. Pretty soon, you can begin to use the word **heel** when he comes and walks at your side. If he stops, jerk him back firmly and say **heel.** If he bounds ahead, do the same thing and praise him when he comes back. Before you know it, he will be marching proudly by your side, the perfect gentleman. Of course, be prepared for little mishaps, such as the local cat, another dog, or an auto which may distract your dog before he has thoroughly mastered the commands to **come** and **heel.** Firmness and kindness should prevail, however.

Once you feel that he has thoroughly learned these lessons, try it off the lead. Hints to remember:

1. **Never work with your dog on any lesson until he has re-lieved himself.**
2. **Keep the lessons short. Fifteen minutes at a time is plenty.**

3. **Don't expect a dog to stay at "heel" for the whole walk; after all, he's a dog, isn't he, and a fellow needs a little time to play.**

ADVANCED TRAINING

SIT: Once your dog has learned the above, he is ready for the command to **sit.** You begin by adding the word **down** to his vocabulary. When he comes to you and jumps up, you say **down** and force him down to the ground. Praise him when he obeys. Keep this up until he has learned not to jump up when you begin training.

The next step is **sit.** Stand the dog on your left side with the lead on, and tell him to **sit.** Follow words with action and push his hindquarters down. He may lie down all the way, and then you will just have to haul him up again and push down his hindquarters once more. Should he accidentally or actually begin to **sit,** praise him generously. You can appreciate what a hard lesson this is for him, for all he wants to do is jump up, lap your face and start playing. Repeat the lesson several times a day for short periods. Don't punish; just reward success or partial success with praise.

The command **lie down** can be taught in much the same way. Once the lesson is learned, try it without the lead.

STAY: Your dog now **comes, heels, sits down** and **lies down.** But the minute you leave, he does too! If you can teach him to **stay,** this will prove valuable. Suppose you want him to remain in the car while you shop, or with the baby carriage, or to stay quiet when a friend arrives. He must learn to stay in one place for a short period. Just as with the early lessons, use example and praise. As he learns, increase the scope of the command.

When you first command him to **stay,** sit him down, say **stay,** and then, holding the leash, walk around him or out towards the end of the lead. Of course, he will jump up and follow you. Don't yell at him; simply walk back and force him back into a sitting position, and then say **sit—stay.** You can also use a hand signal. Hold the palm of your hand in front of his nose when you say **sit—stay.** He will learn that as well as the word. After a while, he will get the idea and remain sitting while you walk around him.

When this lesson is learned, you can put the lead on the ground. Perhaps he is again nervous. Hold it with your foot. It won't be too long before you can leave him unattended and walk off. If he bolts

A brace of Dobermans in sit position.

after you, no praise, just repeat the whole lesson again. When you think he is sufficiently trained in the sit-stay position, then try distracting him by running off or bouncing a ball under his nose. Each time, if he gets up and starts off, begin again as before. Once the lesson is over and he has performed well, of course you can pat him and tell him how well he has done. Be careful not to pat him as soon as he has remained sitting for a moment, or he will think that the lesson's over.

The authors believe that if your dog is housebroken and can obey the commands to **come, heel, sit, lie down,** and **stay,** he will be completely manageable. You can then teach him tricks if you wish. If you so desire, teach your puppy to beg by propping him in the proper position and encouraging him to repeat this. Do not, however, allow him to use this cute trick to get food from you at the table. If you wish to reward him with a dog biscuit or candy at the time of the trick, fine, but if you feed him while you are eating because he begs so cutely, this cute trick will only become an chronic nuisance.

SPECIAL PROBLEMS

Some dogs, because of indifferent training or lack of training, develop problems which must be cured before they become acute and dangerous. The dog who jumps on people, barks all night, chases cars, and bites or steals food from the table must be retrained.

Start training your Doberman early in his life, but also provide him with such comforts as this dog bed.

A Doberman should not jump on people

JUMPING ON PEOPLE: There are several ways to combat this. If your dog will not obey your command to get down and not jump you can try the following: start by telling him **no** and putting him firmly on the floor. If he stays down, pat him. Some trainers advocate that when the dog jumps up you catch him with your knee so he falls back. This is unpleasant enough to stop him. Don't let him get the idea you are hurting him deliberately. As soon as he obeys, praise him.

CHASING CARS: There is no more dangerous and annoying habit for a dog than chasing cars. Dogs have been hit that way, and often in an effort to avoid the dog the driver endangers the lives of others. The best method is to start early and instill a proper fear of cars. Have another drive a car as you walk your dog along the road. When the car comes along, the driver is to give several loud blasts on the horn. At the same time you jerk your dog over to the side of the road. Repeat this several times, and the dog will instinctively move over to the side when he hears a car.

For the already delinquent dog, more severe methods must be used. The driver of the car can use a water pistol and squirt water at the dog as he jumps out at the car, or the driver can leap out of the car and yell loudly at the dog. Of course, you should be nearby in case the dog becomes frightened enough to attack the man. Once your dog shows that he has learned his lesson, he really deserves a medal! But a piece of dog candy will probably serve just as well.

BARKING: Many people purchase a dog for use as a watchdog. Persons on farms or valuable property, or those who are alone at night, may want a dog to warn them of approaching strangers. In these cases, the dog's bark is an asset. But the dog who barks all night, or barks at everyone regardless of who he is, or never stops barking at familiar people such as the paper boy, or garbage man, should be trained to be silent. Barking is a dog's way of talking and, of course, you don't want to completely muzzle him. But if you live in an apartment or populous neighborhood, a barking dog is very annoying and he often starts other dogs in the area baying. The resulting night-long chorus can cause troublesome relations with non-dog owners, and even some dog owners whose sleep is affected.

Prevention is the best cure, and you can start early after the basic lessons are completed. Begin by leaving your dog alone in his room. If he starts to bark, yell at him or knock loudly at the door. If he

Ch. Dictator von Glenhugel. Breeder: John Cholley. Owners: Peggy and Bob Adamson. Photo by Marsh.

Canadian Ch. Roger V. Franconia, CD. Owned by Mrs. Ellen Hoffmann.

Mrs. Dino Di Primio's Dobermans prove that two can do it just as easy as one. Shown, a Double Heel with a brace of Dobermans. Both are champions.

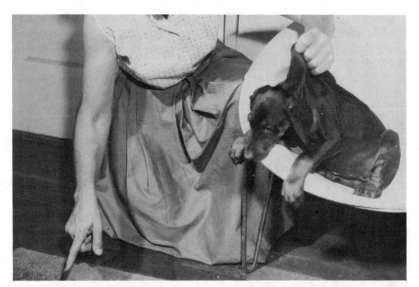

Your puppy should be taught that certain places are not for him. Be firm in your demands.

persists, go in and look your maddest. You can also be sly and pretend to go away. When he begins to howl, go through the routine again.

BITING: Dogs who bite are potentially dangerous. And dogs who continue to bite can be put away by order of a court if there have been complaints. First and foremost, do not encourage your young puppy to bite people, even playfully (and that is what he is doing when he starts, *just playing*). If he must chew on something, get him some inanimate object such as a toy or a rawhide bone. If he continues to bite, express your disapproval. He may need more severe punishment. Hold his jaw shut until he stops or slap him gently on the muzzle. Be sure to fondle him afterwards if he obeys. If you do not tease your dog, he will be less inclined to bite. A dog doesn't like to be poked or interrupted when he is eating. His instincts may cause him to growl and defend himself. But a dog should not growl at his master; firm treatment will tell him so.

FURNITURE SITTING: Do you come home and find your dog in your favorite chair? Next thing you know, he will have your slippers and your paper too. This is a habit which should be broken, unless you don't mind cleaning bills. Remove the dog firmly. Perhaps you can provide a comfortable spot in the living room for him so he can be with you. If it continues, some trainers advocate

137

All work and no play for either boy or dog is not recommended. Buy a special dog toy for your Doberman and he will certainly appreciate it.

setting a little mousetrap under some paper on the chair. The noise will frighten him off. This can be used, but if you are inclined to worry over noses and toes, try a child's squeaky toy or crackly paper. **FOOD STEALING:** Dogs who steal food are both impolite and dangerous to themselves. If your dog does take food he may be eating the wrong foods and ruining that careful diet you prepared, or perhaps he may eat a poisonous substance. Train him to take food only from his dinner plate, at his dinner hour, or on special occasions when you offer a treat. A loud **no** when your dog reaches for forbidden food and general disapproval may work, but you can also try pepper on the enticing tidbit.

Dogs sometimes have other annoying habits which can be cured using much the same methods described above. Kindness and consistency are important and reward for good behavior will reinforce your dog's good habits and discourage bad ones.

SPECIAL TRAINING FOR SHOWING

There are many excellent books on the market describing the type of training you need for showing and obedience trials. One to be

Portable kennels can be taken to a dog show and quickly set up.

The choke collar around the Doberman's neck is an excellent training device.

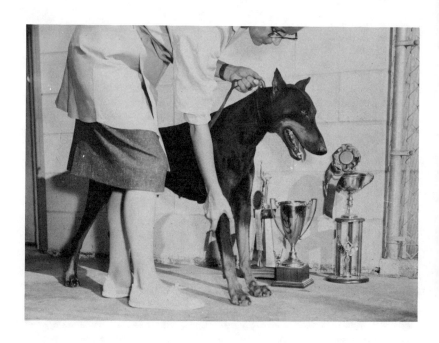

In stacking your Doberman for a show, start with the front legs and end with the hind legs. Practice stacking your Doberman at home so he will become accustomed to the procedure.

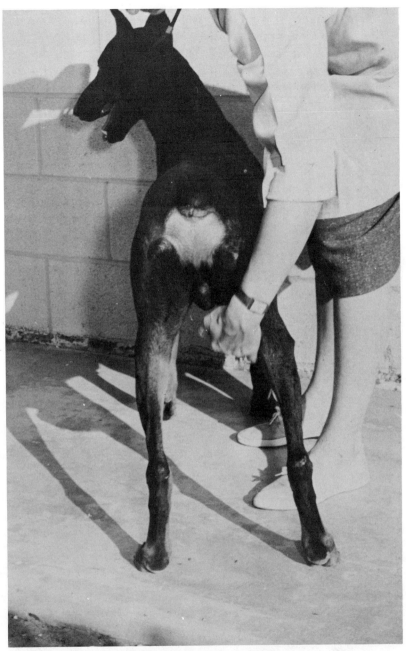

Place each leg in the exact position you want.

highly recommended is the publication **How to Housebreak and Train Your Dog** by Arthur Liebers. This booklet, in addition to basic training, also describes the training needed to qualify for the Obedience Trials of the AKC.

The title of Companion Dog (C.D.) in the Novice Class is awarded if your dog can:

1. Heel on leash
2. Stand for examination by the judge
3. Heel free of the leash
4. Come when called
5. Sit for one minute
6. Sit for three minutes

When this hurdle is passed, your dog is ready to earn his C.D.X. (X for Excellent). This requires that he:

1. Heel free
2. Drop on recall
3. Retrieve on flat (ground)
4. Retrieve over an obstacle
5. Broad jump
6. Sit for three minutes
7. Sit for five minutes

Retrieving over an obstacle is only part of an obedience trial.

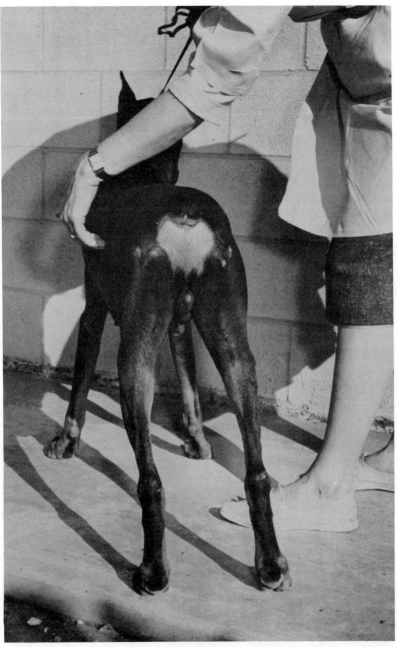

To straighten your Doberman for a show pose, just tap him on the erring side until perfectly straight.

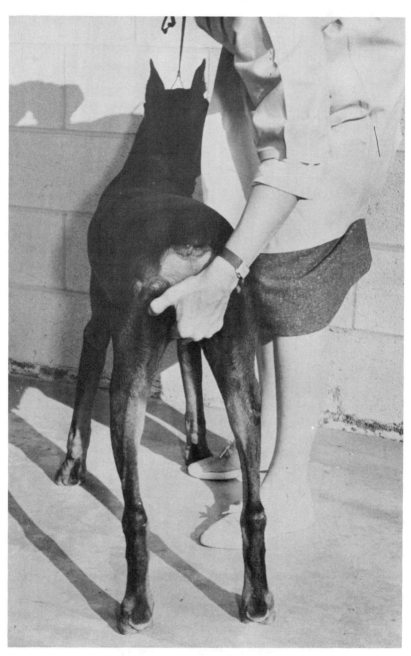

Lift the dog off his feet when stacking for show.

Part of advanced obedience training is the broad jump. Training your Doberman can be fun, and the end result a highly trained companion.

He then enters the Utility Class and can compete in tests including scent discrimination, signal exercises, directed jumping, and group exams. The final test is a tracking exercise, and with that he earns his U.D.T. (T for Tracking), the Ph.D. of the Obedience Class.

DOG TRAINING CLASSES

Many dogs are sent by their owners to professional trainers. This is essential when there is no one at home to supervise a dog and teach him his *p's* and *q's*. Or perhaps the dog is quite large and active and a trainer is necessary. Another reason might be that you plan to show the dog or place him in Obedience Trials, and want professional help. If your dog has been badly trained or frightened, you may want such a person to straighten him out. Be prepared for fees which may be high. Your veterinarian or breeder can probably recommend a trainer, or you can look through the many dog publications. Be sure when you take the dog home that you receive full instructions on how to handle him and the proper words to use.

This Doberman returns the glove to Dino Di Primio in a perfect retrieve.

Ch. Fidelia vom Ahrtal, bred and owned by Tess Hesseler.

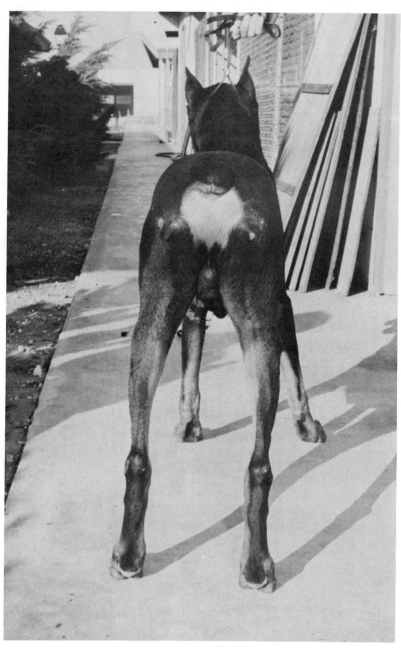

Good straight legs and rear stance are necessary in a show dog.

CLASSES

Many communities sponsor classes for dogs. The local S. P. C. A. or humane society may hold inexpensive classes, or the local dog club may sponsor one. The cost of the classes is generally modest— about $10.00. You will long remember attending the first class of the year in your home town. What bedlam, what a commotion! People and dogs will be pulled all over the place. But by the time the class is under way and in the following weeks, calm, more or less, will reign. You can check with friends or with your veterinarian to see if the classes are effective and the teacher qualified. But don't think that all you will have to do is to attend classes and your dog will be the perfect lady or gentleman. You must be prepared to practice what you *both* have learned when you go home. The advantages of a training class for dogs are that you do obtain the services of a professional who can teach you how to do it, and that the dog becomes accustomed to other dogs and strangers.

Most dogs prefer people to other dogs; they are truly man's companion. But they must learn to respect other dogs and not fight with them. Fights are dangerous both to dogs and the bystanders.

A four-month-old Doberman being taught to stand properly on a show lead.

If your dog does get into a dog fight, don't step in unless you are prepared to get bitten or scratched. He may be so excited that your dog may not even know you. Cold water from a hose is often effective. If you have guts, you can wade in and grab the most aggressive dog. Hold him tightly by the collar or the throat until he is half choked. He will generally let go. Neighbors who cooperate and keep their dogs in, or penned in runs, rarely have these problems.

THE DOBERMAN PINSCHER'S TRAINING

The Doberman has a reputation, in many places, for viciousness. This is untrue. The Doberman has been used extensively in police and army work it is true, but he is perfectly under control then. The Doberman is a one-man dog and generally merely tolerates others around him. He is safe with and protective of children. He makes an excellent watch dog. His training should follow the same general procedures as for other dogs. Because he is a big and strong dog, you may have to jerk his lead a bit harder or pull a little more, but rough treatment will do more harm than good. Never try to train your Doberman in defensive tactics—this should be left to police and army dogs and may cause you grief if used improperly.

To summarize—training is fundamental if you and your Doberman are to live together in harmony. A well-trained dog is both obedient and happy, not cowed or vicious. This can best be accomplished by training him with kindness, firmness, consistency, and the proper rewards for good behavior.

Chapter X
Kennels, Runs and Bedding

A man's home is his castle and a dog's home is his kennel. But your dog depends on *you* to provide him with clean comfortable quarters.

The first thing you must do when your dog arrives is to show him where he lives. This may be a spot in the house or a doghouse outside. But it is his own place. And the first rule is that kennels and bedding must be kept clean and dry. Dirty living quarters can harbor many germs, especially worm eggs which are passed on to the dog.

When your dog arrives, remember that he is in a strange home, far from his family. You have already decided where he is to stay,

Attractive Doberman Pinscher kennel. Not only is it landscaped with shrubs and trees, but it is cleaned regularly to keep it eye-appealing and sanitary.

International Ch. Elfred's Merri-Maker. Shown handling is Mrs. Ellen Hoffmann, judge John Lundberg looks on. Sire: Ch. Steb's Top Skipper. Dam: Ch. Barlynn's Clean Sweep. Photo by Norton of Kent.

indoors or outdoors. Show him his new home, but don't just leave him there and depart, turning off the light or closing the door. He's young, probably frightened, and very lonely. A little love and affection and time for him to get acquainted and sniff about his bed or kennel and he'll settle in fast enough.

If you live in an apartment, naturally, he will live indoors. If possible, choose a spot that is convenient to the whole family, where the dog can have some privacy. If you live in a house, you have the option of having an indoor or outdoor pet. Most small dogs should be indoors as they have less resistance to weather changes and extremes. A large, active dog is probably better off outdoors in a comfortable house with a large run. But whatever type of housing you provide for your pet, it must be clean, airy, warm in winter, ventilated in summer and large enough to accomodate your dog.

When should a dog be outside? Small puppies warmed by their mothers can huddle outside in a kennel in quite cold weather. If it is very cold, of course, they should be inside, especially if they are

Ch. Damasyn The Solitaire, CDX. Bred and owned by Bob Adamson. Sire: Ch. Dictator von Glenhugel. Dam: Ch. Damasyn The Sultry Sister. Photo by Wm. Brown.

new-born. Older dogs with thick coats and hardy dispositions can stay outdoors. Indeed, it is dangerous to keep an outdoor dog inside for too long. He will be more susceptible to the cold after that.

PROFESSIONAL KENNELS

When you consider a kennel for boarding or hospitalization there are certain factors in kennel construction which you should note, to see if the kennel is satisfactory.

A good kennel is large and airy. The ceiling is high, with good ventilation. The kennel contains pens and sleeping areas adequate for the size dog they accomodate, as well as separate quarters for sick dogs and whelping. Each dog should have his own sleep space, but outdoor pens can be shared for exercise. The kennels should be clean. Some kennels today use wire bottomed pens. These have the advantage of being easier to keep clean and less likely to harbor germs. A wirebottomed pen is made up of two parts: a box for sleeping and an outdoor area for play and exercise. A hinged door provides room to clean and show the dogs. Contrary to what many people think, the wire bottom does not injure the dog's feet.

OUTDOOR KENNELS FOR YOUR DOBERMAN PINSCHER

Most people, however, are concerned with housing a single dog, or two at the most. Outdoor housing can be purchased. If you do buy a doghouse, be sure it is solidly constructed, easy to clean and

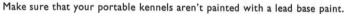

Make sure that your portable kennels aren't painted with a lead base paint.

Ch. Elfred's Spark Plug, bred and owned by Mrs. Ellen Hoffmann. Sire: Ch. Steb's Top Skipper. Dam: Alfred's Doretta. Shown from left to right: Dr. Shute, judge; Mrs. Ellen Hoffmann, handler; club president. Photo by Evelyn M. Shafer.

adequately ventilated. It must be large enough! A small puppy may grow into a large dog. Veterinarians recommend that the sleeping area, your dog's bedroom, be at least two times the width of the grown dog and one and one-half times his height.

Place the kennel in a spot that has some shade as well as sun. If the roof is hinged, you can open it to air the kennel. If possible, place the house a couple of inches off the ground so that moisture and rodents do not affect your dog.

A homemade kennel can be constructed using old lumber and materials from your workshop. Your doghouse should follow the two-room plan—one room for sleeping and an entry way. A porch is nice also, so your dog can watch the world go by without having to lie on wet ground. If you live in a cold climate, the kennel should be insulated. The hinged roof makes it easy to clean.

CAUTION! WHEN YOU PAINT YOUR DOG HOUSE, BE SURE THAT THE PAINT DOES NOT HAVE A LEAD BASE.

Ch. Bailes Bigwig of Gracewood, bred and owned by Mrs. Boyce Bailes. He is being handled by Joe Gregory, while judge Percy Roberts holds ribbon. Photo by Norton of Kent.

Photograph, page 157: Elfred's Mr. Victory, bred by Mrs. Ellen Hoffmann, owned by Mrs. C. A. Bodar. Sire: Tri-international Ch. Elfred's Spark Plug. Dam: K. L's Hella. Mr. Victory is being shown handled by Mrs. Ellen Hoffmann while judge Carl Woods looks on. Photo by W. Bushman.

Better ventilation will be provided if you slant the roof. And you can also provide a slightly raised curbing at the entry of the bedroom, to keep bedding in place.

To keep the kennel clean, scrub it with hot water. A mild disinfectant or diluted Lysol can be used to disinfect the kennel. Your dog is proud of his home and not likely to mess it up, but if he has been sick or just wormed, be sure that the kennel is thoroughly scrubbed and disinfected, and the bedding burned.

The best type of bedding for an outdoor kennel is cedar shavings. Cedar shavings are easily purchased in any pet store, and they smell sweet and clean. Be sure to change the bedding every so often.

INDOOR SLEEPING QUARTERS FOR YOUR DOBERMAN PINSCHER

A dog raised indoors should also have a private place. Sometimes, this may be in the cellar, but only if you are fortunate enough to have a warm dry cellar. Many people use the family room which has less valuable furniture and rugs.

Ch. Stormson's Crashing Baron Jet, bred by Betty Louise Van Bueltzen and owned by Mary D. and Walter J. Quinn. Sire: Ch. Rancho Dobe's Storm. Judge Paul T. Haskell presents ribbon while handler William P. Gilbert holds Baron Jet on lead. Photo by Evelyn M. Shafer.

If you keep your Doberman indoors, buy him a large dog bed for health and comfort.

Most people who provide for their dogs indoors purchase a bed. A trip to the neighborhood pet stores will show the number of commercially available sizes and styles. The two major types are wicker and metal, and which one you choose depends on where you plan to put your dog's bed. If he is to be in the kitchen, bedroom or the family room, the wicker is more attractive. If appearance is no concern the metal is considered sturdier. Be sure that the metal is painted with a paint which does not have a lead base. If you are worried about your puppy chewing up the wicker and getting splinters, there is a harmless, bitter tasting preparation on the market which can be rubbed on the wicker and will discourage chewing.

Two types of filling are used for mattresses: cedar shavings and cotton. The mattresses with cedar shavings can be changed, which may be necessary if you have a small puppy. It may be better, while the dog is young, to provide him with an old blanket which can be chewed to rags. But beware, many dogs become attached to their blanket and won't give it up.

RUNS FOR DOBERMAN PINSCHERS

If you have a city dog, you naturally will take him for walks on a leash. Both master and dog can get their daily constitutional this way. But in the suburbs or country, the best way to exercise your dog is to provide a run for him. One of the problems of the country dog is road safety. Since it is possible to run free—either singly or with groups of other dogs—speeding motorists, wild animals and other natural accidents can endanger his life. The considerate dog owner will provide a place for his dog to exercise when he can't take him out on the leash. The run should be rectangular in shape and as large as possible, up to 20 x 40 feet. Provide a strong wire fence at least 4 feet high, with a gate fastened with a spring hook. If there is no wooden or iron top rail, the dog will be less likely to try to jump over. Dogs usually aim at something when they jump, and if there is only a thin strand of wire at the top he will have no target. The use of tie-out stakes is also to be recommended.

There are many opinions as to the best flooring for runs and kennels. The one basic principle on which all agree is that the material should be easy to keep clean. Some experts recommend concrete, smoothly troweled and finished. Others say that this harbors worm eggs and is very hard to keep clean. Sand is often recommended, but the same argument is used against sand. Grass,

Wash down your Doberman runs at regular intervals. This will aid in keeping the mite and flea population in check.

All metal kennels provide maximum security.

Dog doors like this, or similar to it, are available. See your pet retailer for the kind which will fill your Doberman's needs the best.

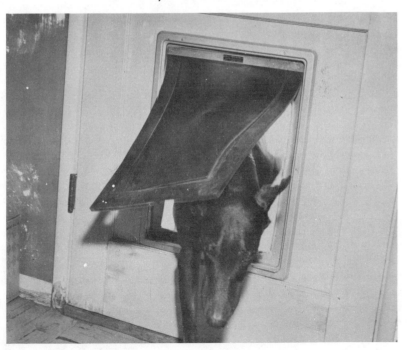

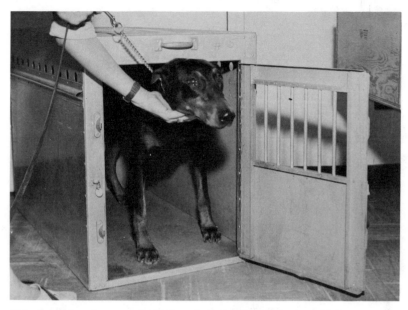

This all-metal carrier can easily be kept clean. Excellent sanitation will always mean a healthier dog.

if your run is not permanent, is satisfactory, but you must expect that it will be considerably trampled.

Some dog owners have the kennel and run together. Others put the dog in the run only for exercise. Protect your dog from the hot sun by providing some shade if there is no doghouse. You can place the run near or under some trees, or construct a platform for protection.

Be sure you provide water also. There is nothing like a fresh drink to cool a fellow off after a hot run around the exercise area. If you do have a run, no matter how large it is, don't leave your pet in for very long stretches. Dogs, like people, get bored and your dog likes a change of scenery, even if he only goes into the house or his kennel.

The major points to remember about housing and runs are that they must be clean and comfortable. This will keep your dog healthier and happier also.

Chapter XI
Grooming and Exercising

There is nothing more beautiful than a healthy, well-groomed Doberman Pinscher with his shining coat, alert eyes and athletic stance. As the preceding chapters have told how to make your Doberman healthy and happy, this chapter will show you how to make his appearance reflect the care you have given to your dog.

As owners of dogs, we know that both we and our dogs delight in compliments. By regular grooming and careful provision for exercising, we can doubly reward our pet with well-earned praise and a happy, healthy life.

Ch. Saltsman's Vint being given final touches for a show.

Ch. Elfred's Spark Plug earned his American, Bermudian, and Canadian championships before he was two years old. Right, judge Louis Murr; left, handler Ellen Hoffmann. Photo by Evelyn M. Shafer.

Ch. Berman Brier, bred and owned by Bernard Berman, shown here being handled by Wm. A. Riemann, while judge R. Cleveland presents honors. Photo by Evelyn M. Shafer.

A good dog brush can be used on a Doberman at least once a week, and daily if possible.

GROOMING

Grooming is a matter of habit for both dog and master. Regular grooming should be a pleasurable occasion for both; it will be, if your pet is accustomed to being combed and brushed. Start the training of your dog early, be kind but firm, and you will find that he will soon begin to enjoy his grooming sessions.

TRAINING FOR PLEASURABLE GROOMING

The first thing to teach your Doberman is *patience* during grooming. Don't let him get away with impatient behavior—after all, who's the boss, anyway?

He must learn to stand quietly while being combed and brushed. This is mostly a matter of starting early in his life. Some breeders begin to brush the pups while they are still in the nest, and as a result have no difficulty when the pups grow up.

Since the best place to groom a dog is on a table or bench, you should train your Doberman Pinscher to jump onto the table or bench, preferably on command. **Table** is the command used by most breeders, and the dog's fondness for grooming will simplify your task.

At the start, or if your pet is nervous (or you are!), attach his leash to a hook above the table or bench. This will hold him in place. If your dog is very young, or nervous, start your grooming activities from the rear, so that he can get accustomed to the new sensations.

YOUR DOBERMAN'S COAT

A dog's coat is a direct reflection of his heredity, diet, and general health, shown to its best by grooming. Proper care of the coat will assure that it is shiny and free from parasites and coat or skin ailments.

The skin and coat of all dogs have certain general characteristics in common. Dogs' skin contain oil glands (which secrete oil to keep the coat shining and waterproof), the sebaceous glands (related to hair growth) and some sweat glands. The sebaceous glands secrete a waxy substance called sebum, which coats the hair as it grows. It is this substance which you may find coating your dog's collar, and sometimes accounts for that "doggy" odor.

The skin of dogs is much like that of human beings, and do not be surprised if your dog occasionally develops dandruff, since the skin continually sheds and renews itself.

A Doberman's coat will glisten if well groomed. Left to right: Ch. Dictator von Glenhugel, Ch. Granda von Palanka, and owner, Peggy Adamson.

Brushing down a Doberman's coat can be pleasurable for all concerned. Your pet shop will have many different types of brushes to select from.

Most breeds of dogs have two coats—a soft undercoat and an outercoat. The Doberman Pinscher does not have an undercoat (he is allowed, by AKC standards, to have an invisible gray undercoat on the neck), which accounts for his sleek look. In any event, dogs generally shed at least once a year, and some seem to shed all year round. We know that the increasing length of daylight hours in spring is one factor causing shedding. Dogs who live primarily indoors and are exposed to artificial light may shed more often or even throughout the year.

COMBING AND BRUSHING

It is a good idea to groom your Doberman at least once a week, or if you have the time, once a day. This will give your dog a shining look. The Doberman is one of the easiest dogs to keep neat and well-groomed, since he is naturally so. Most Dobermans need not be combed before they are brushed, unless they are very dirty. A suitable sturdy comb which will not break or bend can be obtained in any pet store. When combing this short-haired dog, be careful to avoid scraping his skin. If there are any mats, tease them apart; the use of a little oil will make this task easier. Cutting mats leaves an unsightly bald spot. Burrs should also be removed without the use of scissors.

Brush your Doberman carefully after any necessary combing. While most dogs need very stiff brushes, Dobermans need only a moderately stiff brush. Brush in the direction of the coat until it is smooth and shining. A hound glove may be used to give an extra gleam for special occasions. You will find that your dog gets much pleasure from this phase of grooming. Both comb and brush should be cleaned after each use (the comb is helpful in cleaning the brush) and then stored in the open to air out.

NAIL CLIPPING

Long nails can force a dog's toes outward and permanently affect his stance if they occur during puppyhood. If you enjoy an occasional romp with your pet, you will find it safer for both you and your clothing to keep the nails clipped.

Your veterinarian can clip your dog's nails as part of his regular check-up, or you can, with the aid of a pair of special nail clippers for

Clip a puppy's nails with small canine nail clippers. Dog nail clippers can be purchased at your pet shop. Photo by Three Lions, Inc.

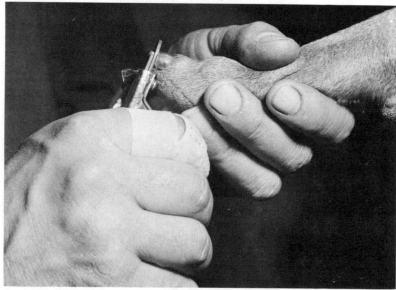

Ch. Willa V. Ahrtal, bred and owned by Tess Henseler. Sire: Ch. Dorian V. Ahrtal, CD. Dam: Ch. Elektra V. Ahrtal, CD. Photo by Wm. Brown.

Elfred's Frieda (Diana) CD, bred by Mrs. Ellen Hoffmann, and owned by Mr. and Mrs. James De Crosta. Photo shows Mrs. De Crosta handling, while judge Seth Campbell holds Elfred's Frieda's new honors.

English Ch. Lustre of Tavey, owned by Mrs. J. Curnow. Photo by C. M. Cooke & Son.

Clipping a Doberman Pinscher's nails can be easy and painless, if you use the right equipment. Visit your pet shop, and let the owner show you several.

Ch. Damasyn The Sonnet, CD. Bred by Peggy Adamson, and owned by Peggy Adamson and Agnes Johnson Eathorne. Sire: Ch. Dictator von Glenhugel. Dam: Damasyn The Song.

dogs. Do it yourself! The part you must trim is the hook, the section of the nail which curves down. Be careful not to cut into the quick (the vein running through the nail), as it bleeds profusely. In small pups or light-haired dogs, the line where the vein begins is easy to spot. The adult Doberman's nails are dark, but shining a flashlight under the nail can help you to spot the quick.

Are you nervous about clipping? Then file the nails. A good file can do an excellent job of shortening nails, or the file can be used to finish the job after the nails are clipped. Your petshop supplies these files.

If you do cut into the dog's toes, it is not tragic—apply a styptic pencil until the bleeding has stopped, then bandage the foot. The bandage helps keep blood from spattering all over the place.

Most people find that their dog's nails need trimming about every two months. But if your dog walks mostly on concrete sidewalks, his nails will wear down naturally, and he may never need clipping.

English Ch. Jupiter of Tavey, owned by Mr. A. B. Hogg. Photo by C. M. Cooke & Son.

Ch. Rhythm of Tavey, owned by the Ministry of Defence, Pakistan Army. Photo by
C. M. Cooke & Son.

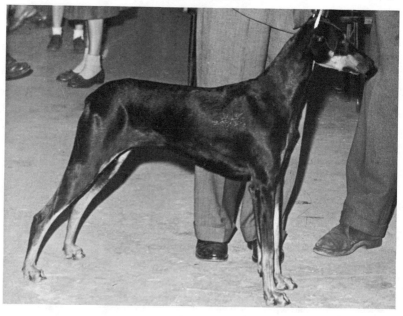

Ch. Elfred's Katrinka, bred by Mrs. Ellen Hoffmann, and owned by Mr. & Mrs. Norton Moore. Sire: Ch. Berman Briar. Dam: Elfred's Doretta. Katrinka is shown being handled by Mrs. Norton Moore, while judge Dr. F. P. Miller holds ribbon. Photo by Nobby De Gravelles.

English Ch. Daybreak of Cartergate, owned by B. J. Taylor. Photo by C. M. Cooke & Son.

TEETH

A little care goes a long way. Tartar is your dog's worst tooth problem. Dog biscuits and bones made from animal hides and nylon are excellent to keep tartar from forming. The authors do not recommend giving meat bones to dogs, even as "toothbrushes." If heavy tartar does form, it can best be removed by a veterinarian.

Sometimes puppy teeth do not fall out on time and must be pulled to make room for the second teeth. Your veterinarian can check for this when your puppy is in for his regular examination.

If your Doberman has "bad breath", check the condition of his mouth and then his diet. There is even a "Happy Breath" available at your petshop to make your dog more "sociable."

EARS

It is best to leave a dog's ears alone. More damage is done by probing than by disease. If your Doberman's ears appear dirty or full of wax, you can clean them out gently with a cotton-tipped swab. But do not thrust the swab into the ear canal.

Check your Doberman's teeth regularly. There are several types of chew products on the market which aid in keeping your dog's teeth clean, plus providing the chewing exercise needed by all dogs.

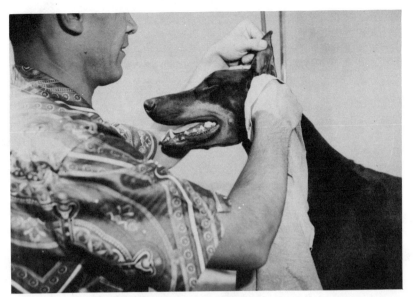
When cleaning your Doberman's ears, be careful. Do not probe.

You may at some time see your dog scratching his ears along the ground or shaking his head violently. He may have some sort of irritation, such as canker, in his ear. Check with your veterinarian. He may recommend that you fill the ear with a preparation such as propylene glycol or mineral oil. To do this, put the dog on a table, hold the ear flap so that you can see the ear canal, and pour the oil into the ear until it is filled. Then massage the base of the ear, wiping up the oil that escapes. This treatment dissolves the wax.

Some dogs have hair growing in the ear canal. This is easily removed by using a forceps or your fingers to pull it out.

EYES

The eyes rarely need grooming care. If they exude a little matter, it is an easy thing to wipe it out with a piece of moist cotton.

ANAL GLANDS

The anal glands are two glands situated on either side of the anus. They appear to serve the same purpose as those of a skunk, and they can also leave an unpleasant odor. If a dog is extremely frightened

English Ch. Satin of Tavey, owned by Mrs. D. Horton. Photo by C. M. Cooke & Son.

English Ch. Francesca of Fulton, owned by Mrs. J. Currie. Photo by C. M. Cooke & Son.

or the loser in a fight, he releases the contents of the glands. The glands may become enlarged and infected if they are not naturally discharged. To prevent infection, they must be emptied from time to time. If your dog begins to drag himself around on his tail and there is a swollen appearance around the anus, check the glands. If you feel two hard lumps, it's time for action.

To empty the glands, stand the dog in a tub or use a big wad of tissue or cotton, as the liquid you will extract is quite smelly. Try not to get any on your hands. With one hand hold the tail up. With the other, using the thumb and middle finger, gently squeeze each lump upward and outward. If this does not empty the glands, they may have to be emptied by a veterinarian.

BATHING

It seems incredible that nearly every puppy owner believes it is wrong to bathe a puppy, or let it get wet, until the pup is six months old. No one likes to advise on such a point because of the usual unscientific method of thinking which causes too many people to feel that because one event follows another, the first is the cause of the second. If you advise a client to bathe her dog and a week later

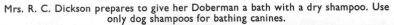
Mrs. R. C. Dickson prepares to give her Doberman a bath with a dry shampoo. Use only dog shampoos for bathing canines.

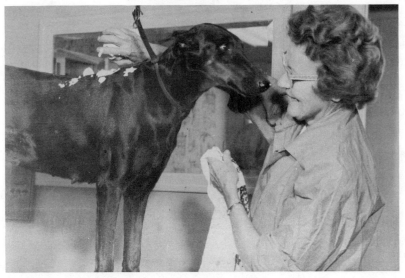

Puppies may be a little skeptical about that first bath, so make it sort of a game. The adult Doberman will take his bath as a matter of course. Whether adult or puppy, dry thoroughly after bathing.

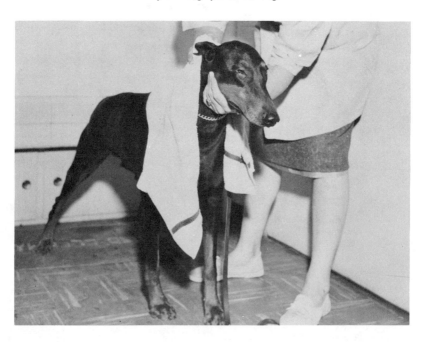

English Ch. Mahadeo Brown Berrie, owned by Mrs. F. and Mr. A. Thompson. Photo by C. M. Cooke & Son.

the pup has pneumonia, you are to blame—you and the bath. Therefore we do not advise you. We can say we've never known of a bath in a warm house, after which the pup was dried, to produce pneumonia, and we have known of hundreds of cases of pneumonia in puppies which had not had baths or been exposed or wet. On the basis of our experience, it is much more likely that a puppy will develop pneumonia if he is not given a bath.

But, to be sensible, we all know that every puppy was born soaking wet and dried from his own body heat and that of his mother's. If one of your puppies gets dirty or smelly, bathe him, not before.

Today there are many ways of bathing puppies. Use special dog soap, cake or liquid. Do not use baby soaps or household soaps, cake or liquid. You can give him a "dry bath" by using a special dog preparation made in any of several ways. These are usually special detergents in which bug-killing drugs are incorporated. Some leave an insecticidal residue; some do not. Some are of a dry, corn-meal powder base, some of foaming whipped-cream consistency.

Bathing is accomplished by selecting a proper place to start with. The size and condition of the puppy help to determine the place. A month-old toy puppy may be washed in a pot, while a six-month-old large size dog needs nothing smaller than the family bathtub. If you don't mind using the tub after the dog, you can use your own. Thousands of dog owners do. Or, if you wish, you can rig up a special tub for your pet.

Some owners wash their dogs standing on the lawn, using a pail of water.

The first thing to do if you are giving a water bath is to get the soap ready. Suppose you decide on flakes. Put a handful of flakes in a pan of warm water and dissolve them. Have another pan with warm water in which is mixed some dog parasite drug, of which several are available. Put a cotton plug in each ear of the pup and he will be less inclined to shake himself. Also put on an apron of some waterproof material to protect yourself in the event the pup struggles or shakes.

The experienced dog washer realizes that water runs off his dog's back and only slowly wets the hair and penetrates to the skin. Soap is a wetting agent. Therefore he soaps the dog as he wets him. Work up a lather by rubbing and rinse the dog thoroughly, making

This Doberman is really lucky to be having his coat dried by an electric dryer.

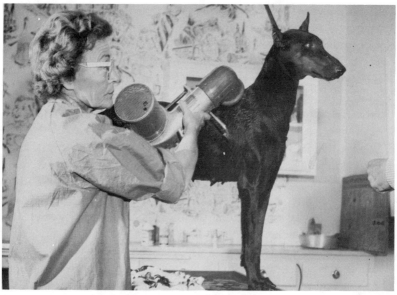

A small animal hair clipper is being used to put last-minute touches on this Doberman's muzzle.

sure that all the soap is washed out of the coat. If there is still dirt to be seen or the odor is not gone, soap and rinse again.

When bathing your dog, squeeze all the water you can from the dog's coat and apply the rinse. This kills any passengers and leaves a clean, fresh odor. Now rub the dog as dry as you can with a towel and leave him where he will finish drying in a warm place.

If you prefer to give him a dry bath, follow directions on the container of whatever you buy. If a coarse powder is used, be sure to comb and brush your dog thoroughly before you allow him his freedom. This method can clean a dog well. If you use a foaming detergent, rub it in and wipe it off thoroughly with a towel. Applying the detergent and dissolving the dirt without removing it does no good, except to kill insects. The dirt is still on the coat, and when the pup is given his freedom he either wipes the dirt off on the rugs, furniture, or your clothes, or else it dries on him and the "bath" proves to be no bath at all.

The matter of drying is really important, especially in cold weather. Many puppy owners wash their charges in the evening, and the pups have to stay inside where it is warm to finish drying.

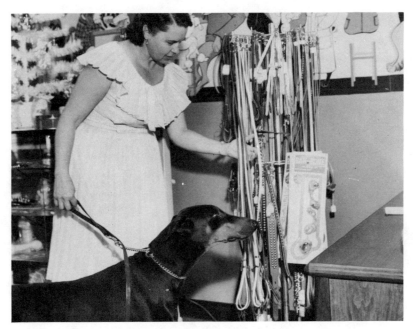

A well-groomed Doberman deserves a new leash and collar.

As puppies grow older, body odors become more pronounced. Ear canker may develop and perfume the air in the puppy's proximity with the odor of bad cheese. The pup's anal glands may become infected and he may slide along your rugs, leaving an obnoxious odor. His collar or harness may accumulate the waxy secretion from his skin and acquire the typical doggy odor.

You can bathe your pup often, but such odors remain to taunt you. However, if you treat the ear canker with what your veterinarian gives you, empty the pup's anal glands occasionally, and scrape the collar, cleansing it with alcohol and then oiling it, the pup will smell sweet and clean after a bath.

Whatever you do, *don't use human products on dogs.* Soaps and shampoos made for humans are too alkaline for dogs' coats and can actually ruin them.

PARASITES

Lice and fleas are discussed in the chapter on diseases (Chapter XII), but oftentimes routine control of these annoying pests can be

English Ch. Carickgreen Walda Negasta, owned by Mr. D. P. Clark. Photo by C. M. Cooke & Son.

English Ch. Talaureen Hurricane, owned by Mrs. E. Barnacle. Photo by C. M. Cooke & Son.

English Ch. Tavey's Stormy Abundance, owned by Mrs. J. Curnow. Photo by C. M. Cooke & Son.

English Ch. Challenger of Sonhende, owned by Mr. R. H. Jackson. Photo by C. M. Cooke & Son.

English Ch. Tumlow Storm Caesar, owned by Mrs. G. F. Platt. Photo by C. M. Cooke & Son.

part of grooming. If you suspect one of these problems, you can bathe your pet with any of the preparations on the market for flea control. Once you spot fleas, be sure to give the kennel and bedding a good bath too. Many professional kennel owners deflea their dogs' quarters regularly. If you keep both dog and bed free from these pests, chances are he won't suffer from them.

SKUNKS

If your dog tangles with a skunk, the skunk will probably be the winner. Unfortunately, both you and the dog are losers. Don't take off in the other direction when he comes home after one of these encounters. Wash him thoroughly and put him near the heat or out in the sun. The odor will disappear in time. Some people advocate washing the animal in tomato juice, but we have not tried this technique as yet.

PAINT

The best chemical with which to remove paint is kerosene. Rub off the paint as soon as possible with a cloth dipped in kerosene, and

English Ch. Tumlow Fantasy, owned by Miss E. Hoxey. Photo by C. M. Cooke & Son.

then wash it off well. Kerosene can burn an animal's skin, so apply it with care.

Keep your Doberman from chewing on paint which is on his fur, as it may contain poisonous substances.

TAR

If the roads in your neighborhood have been recently tarred, rest assured that your dog will have investigated. He may then come home with tar on his feet or coat. To remove tar, wipe off the tar with kerosene, as noted above. It may take several treatments. Fortunately, the Doberman's sleek, short coat minimizes paint and tar problems.

EXERCISE

Exercise is "doing what comes naturally" for most Dobermans. If left completely free, your dog could be found running over the fields and woods. But crowded urban areas and their special requirements of breeding and control impose restrictions on a dog's exercising.

English Ch. Tavey's Stormy Wonder, owned by Mrs. J. Curnow. Photo by C. M. Cooke & Son.

English Ch. Tavey's Stormy Nugget, owned by Mr. F. Williams. Photo by C. M. Cooke & Son.

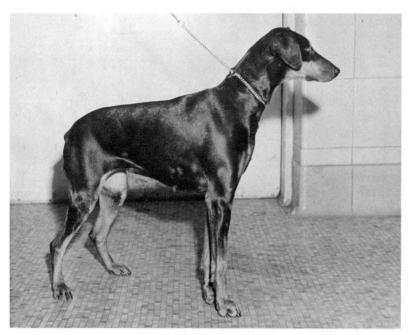

English Ch. Tavey's Stormy Adagio, owned by Mrs. J. Curnow. Photo by C. M. Cooke & Son.

English Ch. Tumlow Fantasy, owned by Miss E. Hoxey. Photo by C. M. Cooke & Son.

English Ch. Tavey's Stormy Wrath, owned by Mrs. J. Curnow. Photo by C. M. Cooke & Son.

The Doberman in the city should be exercised regularly by walking, which he will greatly enjoy. Most cities and towns require that dogs be on a leash when out in the street, but this should not prevent your dog from getting the full benefit from the walk. He will get the rest of his exercise in the house or apartment playing with you or the children of the household, or with his toys.

Even dogs as large as the Doberman Pinscher can get enough exercise in what seems to be a limited space. In a kennel, a run of 10×25 feet is adequate.

The Doberman in the country has much more freedom and can be left to run free for his exercise. However, the authors believe that a run is better than complete freedom (especially if you plan to breed your pet). A run does not rule out walks or an occasional session in the woods and fields. One of the larger dogs in our neighborhood spends the winter towing kids on an old-fashioned sled. Many dogs enjoy swimming and gleefully jump into the water in pursuit of a ball or stick, or simply to chase a friend.

English Ch. Cordelia of Trevellis, owned by Mr. C. W. Starns. Photo by C. M. Cooke & Son.

English Ch. Jove of Cartergate, owned by Miss E. M. Would. Photo by C. M. Cooke & Son.

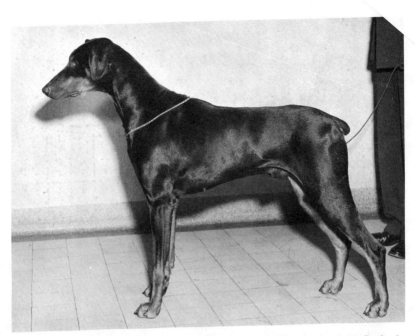

English Ch. Acclimation of Tavey, owned by Mrs. J. Curnow. Photo by C. M. Cooke & Son.

If you have a puppy you may want playthings to distract him from your shoes or chairs. Most pet stores carry a supply of toys which are safe for dogs. Just be careful with rubber toys; see to it that your energetic puppy does not tear them apart and eat the pieces. Toys are not on his diet list! The safest toys are the natural rawhide "bones" offered at most petshops. Nylon "bones" with natural scents are also very valuable.

If you give your dog adequate exercise and proper grooming, diet, and medical care, he will reward you with compliments from the neighbors and perhaps even a blue ribbon at the dog show!

Chapter XII
Diseases and First Aid

The dog is heir to many illnesses, and, as with man, it seems that when one dread form has been overcome by some specific medical cure, another quite as lethal takes its place. It is held by some that this cycle will always continue, since it is Nature's basic way of controlling population.

There are, of course, several ways to circumvent Dame Nature's lethal plans. The initial step in this direction is to put the health of your dog in the hands of one who has the knowledge and equipment to cope competently with canine health problems. We mean, of course, a modern veterinarian. Behind this man are years of study and experience and a knowledge of all the vast research, past and present, which has developed the remarkable cures and artificial immunities that have so drastically lowered the canine mortality rate.

Timely inoculations can prevent many dog diseases.

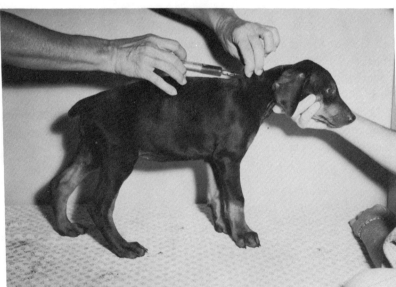

English Ch. Annastock Lance, owned by Mrs. L. J. Parkes. Photo by C. M. Cooke & Son.

English Ch. Tavey's Stormy Leprechaun, owned by Mr. E. Protheroe. Photo by C. M. Cooke & Son.

English Ch. Bowesmoor Mona, owned by Mr. G. D. Thompson. Photo by C. M. Cooke & Son.

English Ch. Auldrigg Corsair, owned by W. Gallaher. Photo by C. M. Cooke & Son.

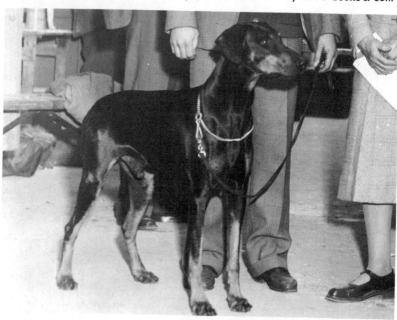

When visiting the veterinarian for the first time, the wise Doberman owner will accompany her pet and console him if need be.

Put your trust in the qualified veterinarian and "beware of Greeks bearing gifts." Beware, too, of helpful friends who say, "I know what the trouble is and how to cure it. The same thing happened to my dog." Home doctoring by unskilled individuals acting upon the advice of unqualified "experts" has killed more dogs than distemper.

Your puppy is constantly exposed to innumerable diseases transmitted by flying and jumping insects, parasites, bacteria, fungus and virus. His body develops defenses and immunities against many of these diseases, but there are many more which we must cure (or immunize him against) if we want him to live his full span.

You are not qualified to treat your dog for many illnesses with the skill or knowledge necessary for success. This book can only give you a resume of modern findings on the most prevalent diseases and illnesses so that you can, in some instances, eliminate them or the causative agent by yourself. Even more important, this chapter will help you recognize disease symptoms in time to seek the aid of your veterinarian.

Many illnesses have an incubation period, during the early stages of which the animal himself may not show the symptoms of the disease, but can readily infect other dogs with which he comes in contact. It is readily seen, then, that places where many dogs are gathered together are particularly dangerous to your dog's health.

Parasitic diseases, which we will first consider, must not be taken too lightly, though they are the easiest of the diseases to cure. Great suffering and even death can come to your pup through these parasites if you neglect to realize the importance of both cure and the control of reinfestation.

EXTERNAL PARASITES

The lowly flea is one of the most dangerous insects from which you must protect your dog. It carries and spreads tapeworm, heartworm and bubonic plague, causes loss of coat and weight, spreads skin disease, and brings untold misery to its poor host. These pests are particularly difficult to combat because their eggs—of which they lay thousands—can lie dormant for months, hatching when conditions of moisture and warmth are present. Thus you may think you have rid your dog (and your house) of these devils, only to find that they mysteriously reappear as weather conditions change.

A veterinarian administers liquid medicine with a paper cup. It is best to never take unnecessary chances.

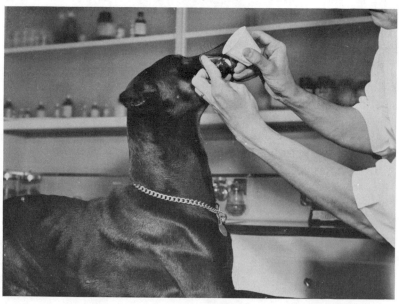

English Ch. Tavey's Stormy Achievement, owned by Mrs. J. Curnow. Photo by C. M. Cooke & Son.

English Ch. Caliph of Trevellis, owned by E. C. Plumb. Photo by C. M. Cooke & Son.

English Ch. Caprice of Cartergate, owned by T. N. Naisby. Photo by C. M. Cooke & Son.

English Ch. Juno of Tavey, owned by Mrs. P. Thorne-Dunn. Photo by C. M. Cooke & Son.

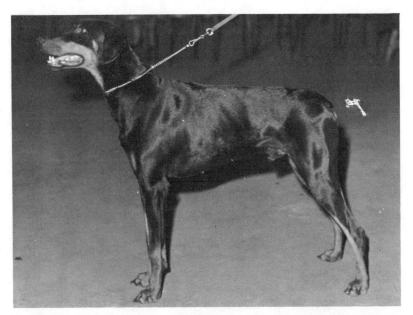

English Ch. Claus of Cartergate, owned by Mrs. P. Thorne-Dunn. Photo by C. M. Cooke & Son.

When your dog has fleas, use any good commercial flea powder which contains fresh rotenone. Dust him freely with the powder. It is not necessary to cover the dog completely, since the flea is active and will quickly reach a spot saturated with the powder and die. Rotenone is also fatal to lice. A solution of this drug in pine oil and added to water to be employed as a dip or rinse will kill all insects except ticks. DDT in liquid soap is excellent and long-potent, its effects lasting for as long as a week. Benzene hexachloride, chlordane, and any number of many new insecticides developed for the control of flies are also lethal to fleas. Whatever specific you use should also be used on your dog's sleeping quarters as well as on the animal itself. Repeat the treatment in ten days to eliminate fleas which have been newly hatched from dormant eggs.

TICKS

There are many kinds of ticks, all of which go through similar stages in their life process. At some stage in their lives they all find it necessary to feed on blood. Luckily, these little vampires are fairly

English Ch. Reichart Judy, owned by Mrs. M. Porterfield. Photo by C. M. Cooke & Son.

easily controlled. The female of the species is much larger than the male, which will generally be found hiding under the female. Care must be taken in the removal of these pests to guard against the mouth parts remaining embedded in the host's skin when the body of the tick is removed. DDT is an effective tick remover. Ether or nail-polish remover, touched to the individual tick, will cause it to relax its grip and fall off the host. The heated head of a match from which the flame has been just extinguished, employed in the same fashion, will cause individual ticks to release their hold and fall from the dog. After veterinary tick treatment, no attempt should be made to remove the pests manually, since the treatment will cause them to drop by themselves as they succumb.

MITES

There are three basic species of mites that generally infect dogs, the demodectic mange mite (red mange), the sarcoptic mange mite (white mange), and the ear mite. Demodectic mange is generally

200

English Ch. Adoration of Dumbrill, owned by Mr. M. B. Theobald. Photo by C. M. Cooke & Son.

English Ch. Caliph of Barrimilne, owned by M. Fagot. Photo by C. M. Cooke & Son.

English Ch. Tavey's Stormy Objection, owned by M. Ferraro-Cini. Photo by C. M. Cooke & Son.

recognized by balding areas on the face, cheeks, and the front parts of the foreleg, which present a moth-eaten appearance. Reddening of the skin and great irritation occurs as a result of the frantic rubbing and scratching of affected parts by the animal. Rawness and thickening of the skin follows. Not too long ago this was a dread disease in dogs, from which few recovered. It is still a persistent and not easily cured condition unless promptly diagnosed and diligently attended to.

Sarcoptic mange mites can infest you as well as your dog. The resulting disease is known as scabies. This disease very much resembles dry dermatitis, or what is commonly called "dry eczema." The coat falls out and the denuded area becomes inflamed and itches constantly.

Ear mites, of course, infest the dog's ear and can be detected by an accumulation of crumbly dark brown or black wax within the ear. Shaking of the head and frequent scratching at the site of the infestation accompanied by squeals and grunting also is symptomatic of the presence of these pests. Canker of the ear is a condition, rather than a specific disease, which covers a wide range of ear infection and which displays symptoms similar to ear mite infection.

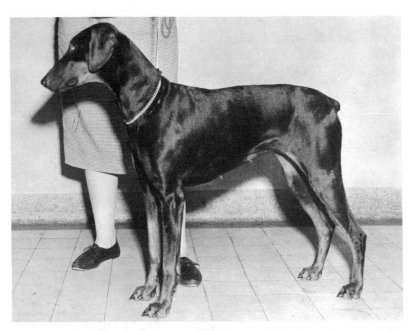

English Ch. Tavey's Stormy Daughter, owned by Mr. E. Protheroe. Photo by C. M. Cooke & Son.

English Ch. Adges Going Places, owned by Miss J. Skinner and Mr. M. Menzies. Photo by C. M. Cooke & Son.

English Ch. Sheumac Storm, owned by Mr. G. A. Tunnicliffe. Photo by C. M. Cooke & Son.

English Ch. Xel of Tavey, owned by Mrs. A. Bastable. Photo by C. M. Cooke & Son.

English Ch. Day of Cartergate, owned by Mr. A. W. Pulley. Photo by C. M. Cooke & Son.

All three of these diseases and ear canker should be treated by your veterinarian. By taking skin scrapings or wax particles from the ear for microscopic examination, he can make an exact diagnosis and recommend specific treatment. The irritations caused by these ailments, unless immediately controlled, can result in loss of appetite and weight, and so lower your dog's natural resistance that he is open to the attack of other diseases which his bodily defenses could normally battle successfully.

INTERNAL PARASITES

It seems strange, in the light of new discovery of specific controls for parasitism, that the incidence of parasitic infestation should still be almost as great as it was years ago. This can only be due to lack of realization by the dog owner of the importance of initial prevention and control against reinfestation. Strict hygiene must be adhered to if pups are not to be immediately reinfested. This is particularly true where worms are concerned.

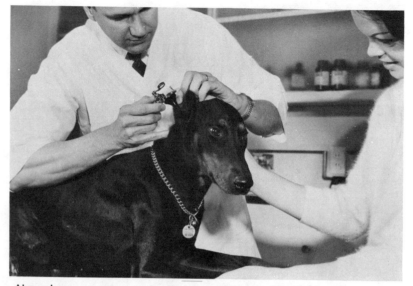
Always let a competent veterinarian treat ear diseases. Chances are excellent that a well-intentioned Doberman owner will do more harm than good, should he try to give treatment to this part of the dog's anatomy.

In attempting to rid our dogs of worms, we must not be swayed by amateur opinion. The so-called "symptoms" of worms may be due to many other reasons. We may see the actual culprits in the animal's stool, but even then it is not wise to worm indiscriminately. The safest method to pursue is to take a small sample of your puppy's stool to your veterinarian. By a fecal analysis he can advise just what specific types of worms infest your dog and what drugs should be used to eliminate them.

Do not worm your puppy because you "think" he should be wormed, or because you are advised to do so by some self-confessed "authority." Drugs employed to expel worms can prove highly dangerous to your pup if used indiscriminately and carelessly, and in many instances the same symptoms that are indicative of the presence of internal parasites can also be the signs of some other affliction.

A word here in regard to that belief that garlic will "cure" worms. Garlic is an excellent flavoring agent, favored by gourmets the world over—but—it will not rid your dog of worms. Its only curative power lies in the fact that, should you use it on a housedog who has worms, the first time he pants in your face you will definitely be cured of ever attempting this pseudo-remedy again.

English Ch. Bridget of Upend, owned by Mrs. Y. Willett. Photo by C. M. Cooke & Son.

English Ch. Baba Black Pepper, owned by Miss E. Hoxey. Photo by C. M. Cooke & Son.

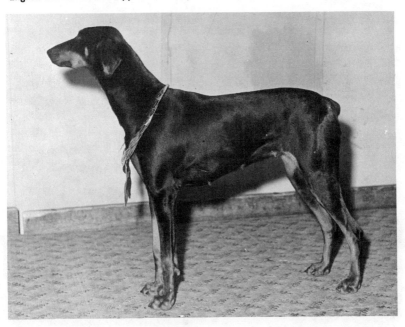

Keeping a Doberman clean and well groomed at all times will also aid in preventing him from being the host of many parasites.

Part of your job in keeping your dog free of external parasites is regular foot cleaning and care. Use special dog nail clippers for this part of grooming.

English Ch. Alli of Girton, owned bv H. Greenhalgh   Photo by C. M. Cooke & Son.

ROUNDWORM

These are the most common worms found in dogs and can have grave effects upon puppies, which they almost invariably infest. Potbellies, general unthriftiness, diarrhea, coughing, lack of appetite, anemia, are the symptoms. They can also cause verminous pneumonia when in the larval stage. Fecal examinations of puppy stools should be made by your veterinarian frequently if control of these parasites is to be constant. Although, theoretically, it is possible for small puppies to be naturally worm free, actually most pups are born infested or contract the parasitic eggs at the mother's teat.

The roundworm lives in the intestine and feeds on the pup's partially digested food, growing and laying eggs which are passed out in the pup's stool to be picked up by him in various ways and so cause reinfestation. The life history of all the intestinal worms is a vicious circle, with the dog the beginning and the end host. This worm is yellowish-white in color and is shaped like a common garden worm, pointed at both ends. It is usually curled when found in the stool. There are several different species of this type of worm. Some

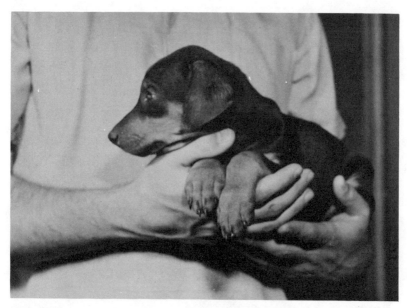

Part of keeping your Doberman healthy is to hold him correctly when he is still a puppy. Photograph shows the proper way.

Most American Dobermans undergo the minor operation of ear cropping.

English Ch. Venture of Vreda, owned by Mr. & Mrs. W. D. Thatcher. Photo by C. M. Cooke & Son.

varieties are more dangerous than others. They discharge toxin within the pup, and the presence of larvae in important internal sections of the pup's body can cause death.

The two drugs most used by kennel owners for the elimination of roundworms are N-butyl-chloride and tetrachloroethylene, but there are a host of other drugs, new and old, that can also do the job efficiently. With most of the worm drugs, give no food to the dog for twenty-four hours, or in the case of puppies, twenty hours, previous to the time he is given the medicine. It is absolutely essential that this starvation limit be adhered to, particularly if the drug used is tetrachloroethylene, since the existence of the slightest amount of food in the stomach or intestine can cause death. One tenth c.c. to each pound of the animal's weight is the dosage for tetrachloroethylene, followed in one hour with a milk-of-magnesia physic, *never* an oily physic. Food may be given two hours later.

N-butyl-chloride is less toxic if the pup has eaten some food during the supposed starvation period. The dosage is one c.c. for every ten pounds of the weight of the dog. Any safe physic may be administered an hour later, and the pup fed within two hours afterward. Large doses of this drug can be given grown dogs without danger, and will kill whipworms as well as roundworms. A second treatment should follow in two weeks. The effect of N-butyl-chloride is cumulative; therefore, when a large dosage is necessary, the total amount to be given can be divided into many small doses administered, one small dose at a time, over a period of hours. The object of this procedure is to prevent the dog from vomiting up the drug, which generally occurs when a large dose is given all at once. This method of administering the drug has been found to be very effective.

HOOKWORMS

These tiny leeches who live on the blood of your dog, which they get from the intestinal walls, cause severe anemia, groaning, fits, diarrhea, loss of appetite and weight, rapid breathing, and swelling of the legs. The same treatment used to eradicate roundworms will also expel hookworms.

Good food is essential for quick recovery, with added amounts of liver and raw meat incorporated in the diet. Blood transfusions are

Good commercial dog food is the key to recovery from hookworm infestation.

Meadowmist Isis of Ahrtal, a great producer, was the dam of seventeen champions. She was bred by Virginia Knauer, and was owned by Tess Henseler. Sire: Ch. Emperor of Marienland. Dam: Dow's Ditty of Marienland.

often necessary if the infestation has been heavy. If one infestation follows another, a certain degree of immunity to the effects of the parasite seems to be built up by the dog. A second treatment should be given two weeks following the initial treatment.

WHIPWORMS

These small, thin whiplike worms are found in the intestines and the caecum. Those found in the intestines are reached and killed by the same drugs used in the eradication of roundworms and hookworms. Most worm medicines will kill these helminths if they reach them, but those which live in the caecum are very difficult to reach. They exude toxins which cause debilitation, anemia, and allied ills, and are probably a contributing factor in lowering the resistance to the onslaught of other infections. The usual symptoms of worm infestation are present.

N-butyl-chloride, in dosage three times greater than the roundworm dosage, appears to be quite effective in reaching the caecum

Dobermans are world travelers, too. These two, Damasyn The Shawn (left), and Damasyn The Aurien (right), are on their way to their new owner, Prince Bhanuband Yukol. At the extreme right is Peggy Adamson, breeder and shipper of these fine Dobermans. Photo by Pan American World Airways.

American and Canadian Ch. Damasyn The Elf, bred and owned by Helen F. Kamerer. Sire: Ch. Dictator von Glenhugel. Dam: Damasyn The April Rain. Photo by Norton of Kent.

and ridding the grown dog of most of these pests. The drug is to be given following the twenty-four hour period of fasting. Administration of an anti-emetic is generally indicated to keep the dog from disgorging the drug.

Hydrogen peroxide administered as an enema is highly effective but very dangerous, and should be applied only by expert hands.

TAPEWORMS

Tapeworms are not easily diagnosed by fecal test, but are easily identified when visible in the dog's stool. The worm is composed of two distinct parts, the head and the segmented body. It is pieces of the segmented body that we see in the stools of the dog. They are usually pink or white, and flat. The common tapeworm, which is most prevalent in our dogs, is about eighteen inches long, and the larvae are carried by the flea. The head of the worm is smaller than a pinhead and attaches itself to the intestinal wall. Contrary to general belief, the puppy infested with tapeworms does not possess an enormous appetite—rather it fluctuates from good to poor. The animal shows the general signs of worm infestation. Often he squats and drags his hindquarters on the ground. This is due to tapeworm larvae moving and wriggling in the lower bowels. One must be careful in diagnosing this symptom, as it may also mean that the dog is suffering from distended anal glands.

Arecolene is an efficient expeller of tapeworms. Dosage is approximately one-tenth grain for every fifteen pounds of the dog's weight, administered after twenty hours of fasting. Nemural is also widely used. One pill for every eight pounds of body weight is given in a small amount of food after twelve hours of starvation. No worm medicine can be considered 100 percent effective in all cases. If one drug does not expel the worms satisfactorily, then another must be tried.

HEARTWORM

This villain inhabits the heart and is the most difficult to treat. The worm is about a foot long and literally stuffs the heart of the affected animal. It is prevalent in the southern states and has long been the curse of sporting-dog breeds. The worm is transmitted principally through the bite of an infected mosquito, which can fly from an infected southern canine visitor directly to your dog and do its dire deed.

Should your Doberman fall victim to ear canker, have your veterinarian do the doctoring, and as quickly as possible.

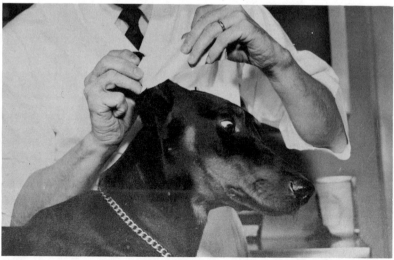

Both kennels and carriers must be kept scrupulously clean in the war against infestation.

The symptoms are: fatigue, gasping, coughing, nervousness, and sometimes dropsy and swelling of the extremities. Treatment for heartworms definitely must be left in the hands of your veterinarian. A wide variety of drugs are used in treatment. The most commonly employed are the arsenicals, antimony compounds, and caracide. Danger exists during cure when dying adult worms move to the lungs, causing suffocation, or when dead adult worms, in a heavily infested dog, block the small blood vessels in the heart muscles. The invading microfilariae are not discernible in the blood until nine months following introduction of the disease by the bite of the carrier mosquito.

In an article on this subject in *Field and Stream* magazine, Joe Stetson describes a controlled experiment in which caracide was employed in periodic treatments as a preventive of heartworm. The experiment was carried out over a period of eighteen months, during which time the untreated dogs became positive for heartworm and eventually died. A post mortem proved the presence of the worm. The dogs that underwent scheduled prophylaxis have been found, by blood test, to be free of circulating microfilariae and are thriving.

This little Blue Doberman puppy needs your help if he is to reach his full potential. Give him the professional medical care he deserves, when needed, and let his well-balanced commercial diet not be lacking. If given the proper care and food, he'll probably grow up to be a champion.

Proper shelters will do much to curb the menace of parasites.

COCCIDIOSIS

This disease is caused by a single-celled protozoa. It affects dogs of all ages, but is not dangerous to mature animals. When puppies become infected by a severe case of coccidiosis, it very often proves fatal, since it produces such general weakness and emaciation that the puppy has no defense against other invading harmful organisms. Loose and bloody stools are indicative of the presence of this disease, as is loss of appetite, weakness, emaciation, discharge from the eyes, and a fever of approximately 103 degrees. The disease is contracted directly or through flies that have come from infected quarters. Infection seems to occur over and over again, limiting the puppy's chance of recovery with each succeeding infection. The duration of the disease is about three weeks, but new infestations can stretch this period of illness on until your puppy has little chance to recover. Strict sanitation and supportive treatment of good nutrition—utilizing milk, fat, kaopectate, and bone ash with added dextrose and calcium—seem to be all that can be done in the way of treatment. Force feed the puppy if necessary. The more food that you can get into him to give him strength until the disease has run its course, the better will be his chances of recovery. Specific cures have been developed in other animals and poultry, but not as yet in dogs.

SKIN DISEASES

Diseases of the skin in dogs are many, varied, and easily confused by the puppy owner. All skin afflictions should be immediately diagnosed and treated by your veterinarian. Whatever drug is prescribed must be employed diligently, and in quantity, and generally long after surface indications of the disease have ceased to exist. A surface cure may be attained, but the infection remains buried deep in the hair follicles or skin glands, to erupt again if treatment is suspended too soon. Contrary to popular belief, diet, if well balanced and complete, is seldom the cause of skin disease.

Eczema

The word "eczema" is a much-abused word, as is the word "dermatitis." Both are used with extravagance in the identification of various forms of skin disorders. We will concern ourselves with the

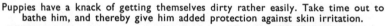

Puppies have a knack of getting themselves dirty rather easily. Take time out to bathe him, and thereby give him added protection against skin irritation.

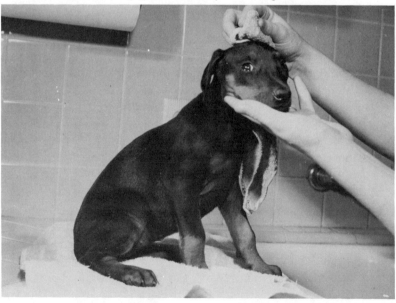

Free of skin disease, this Doberman's coat glistens because the owner fed him properly and groomed his coat daily.

two most prevalent forms of so-called eczema, namely wet eczema and dry eczema. In the wet form, the skin exudes moisture and then scabs over, due to constant scratching and biting by the dog at the site of infection. The dry form manifests itself in dry patches which irritate and itch, causing great discomfort to the dog. In both instances the hair falls out and the spread of the disease is rapid. The cause of these diseases is not yet known, though many are thought to be originated by various fungi and aggravated by allergic conditions. The quickest means of bringing these diseases under control is through the application of a good skin remedy often combined with a fungicide, which your veterinarian will prescribe. An over-all dip, employing specific liquid medication, is beneficial in many cases and has a continuing curative effect over a period of days.

Ringworm

This infection is caused by a fungus and is highly contagious to humans. In the dog it generally appears on the face as a round or oval spot from which the hair has fallen. Ringworm is easily cured by the application of iodine and glycerine (50 per cent of each ingredient) or a fungicide liberally applied. The new antibiotic Malucidin eliminates ringworm quickly and effectively.

Acne

Your puppy will frequently display small eruptions on the soft skin of his belly. These little pimples rupture and form a scab. The rash is caused by inflammation of the skin glands and is not a serious condition. Treatment consists of washing the affected area with alcohol or witch hazel, followed by the application of a healing lotion or powder.

Hookworm Larvae Infection

The skin of your pup can become infected from the eggs and larvae of the hookworm acquired from a muddy hookworm-infested run. The larvae becomes stuck to his coat with mud and burrow into the skin, leaving ugly raw red patches. One or two baths in warm water to which an antiseptic has been added usually cures the condition quickly.

DEFICIENCY DISEASES

These diseases, or conditions, are caused by dietary deficiencies or some condition which robs the diet of necessary ingredients.

Keep the Doberman's ear rack clean to protect him from possible infections.

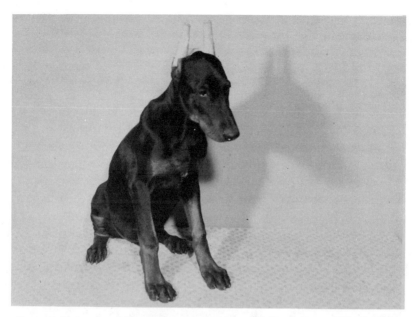

Ears should be cropped by a veterinarian to insure that every possible hygienic precaution has been taken.

Anemia, a deficiency condition, is a shortage of hemoglobin. Hookworms, lice, and any disease that depletes the system of red blood cells, are contributory causes. A shortage or lack of specific minerals or vitamins in the diet can also cause anemia. Not so long ago, rickets was the most common of the deficiency diseases, caused by a lack of one or more of the dietary elements—vitamin D, calcium, and phosphorus. There are other types of deficiency diseases originating in dietary inadequacy and characterized by unthriftiness in one or more phases. The cure exists in supplying the missing food factors to the diet. Sometimes, even though all the necessary dietary elements are present in the food, some are destroyed by improper feeding procedure. For example, a substance in raw eggs, avertin, destroys biotin, one of the B-complex group of vitamins. Cooking will destroy the avertin in the egg white and prevent a biotin deficiency in the diet.

BACTERIAL DISEASES

In this group we find leptospirosis, tetanus, pneumonia, strep infections and many other dangerous diseases. The mortality rate is generally high in all of the bacterial diseases, and treatment should be left to your veterinarian.

Leptospirosis

Leptospirosis is spread most frequently by the urine of infected dogs, which can infect for six months or more after the animal has recovered from the disease. Rats are the carriers of the bacterial agent which produces this disease. A puppy will find a bone upon which an infected rat has urinated, chew the bone, and become infected with the disease in turn. Leptospirosis is primarily dangerous in the damage it does to the kidneys. Complete isolation of affected individuals to keep the disease from spreading and rat control are the chief means of prevention. Also, newly developed vaccines may be employed by your veterinarian as a preventive measure. Initial diagnosis is difficult, and the disease has generally made drastic inroads before a cure is effected. It has been estimated that fully 50 percent of all dogs throughout the world have been stricken with leptospirosis at one time or another and that in many instances the disease was not recognized for what it was. The disease produced by *Leptospira* in the blood of humans is known as Weil's disease.

Your veterinarian is best qualified to diagnose and treat your dog.

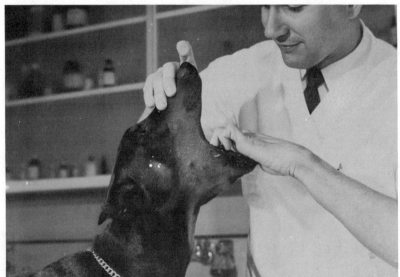

Modern, clean kennels will do much to keep disease and parasites at a minimum.

Tetanus

Lockjaw bacteria produce an exceedingly deadly poison. The germs grow in the depths of a sealed-over wound where oxygen cannot penetrate. To prevent this disease, every deep wound acquired by your dog should be thoroughly cleansed and disinfected, and an antitoxin given the animal. Treatment follows the same general pattern as prevention. If the jaw locks, intravenous feeding must be given.

Strep throat

This is a very contagious disease caused by a specific group of bacteria labeled "streptococcus." Characteristic of this disease is the high temperature that accompanies infection (104 to 106 degrees). Other symptoms are loose stool at the beginning of the disease and a slight optic discharge. The throat becomes intensely inflamed, swallowing is difficult, and the glands under the ears are swollen. Immunity is developed by the host after the initial attack.

Tonsillitis

Inflammation of the tonsils can be either of bacterial or virus origin. It is not a serious disease in itself, but is often a symptom of other diseases. Tonsillitis is not to be confused with strep throat, which is produced by an entirely different organism. The symptoms of tonsillitis are enlarged and reddened tonsils, poor appetite, vomiting, and optic discharge. The disease usually runs its course in from five to seven days. Penicillin, aureomycin, terramycin, chloromycetin, etc., have been used with success in treatment.

Pneumonia

Pneumonia is a bacterial disease of the lungs of which the symptoms are poor appetite, optic discharge, shallow and rapid respiration. Affected animals become immune to the particular type of pneumonia from which they have recovered. Oral treatment utilizing antibiotic or sulfa drugs, combined with a pneumonia jacket of cloth or cotton padding wrapped around the chest area, seems to be standard treatment.

VIRAL DISEASES

The dread viral diseases are caused by the smallest organisms known to man. They live in the cells and often attack the nerve tissue.

Preventive medicine is one of the surest ways to keep your Doberman in excellent health.

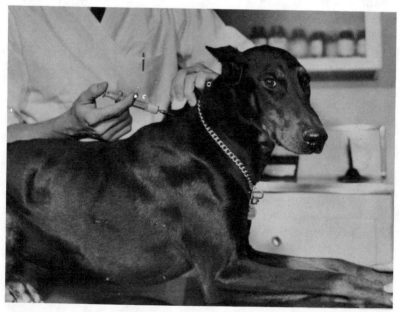

A healthy Doberman is an excellent companion. It is the owner's responsibility to safeguard the Doberman's health.

The tissue thus weakened is easily invaded by many types of bacteria. Complications then set in, and it is these accompanying ills which usually prove fatal. The secondary infections can be treated with several of the "wonder" drugs, and excellent care and nursing is necessary if the stricken animal is to survive. Your veterinarian is the only person qualified to aid your pup when a viral disease strikes. The diseases in this category include distemper, infectious hepatitis, rabies, kennel cough, housedog disease, and primary encephalitis—the latter actually inflammation of the brain, a condition characterizing several illnesses, particularly those of viral origin.

Distemper

Until recently a great many separate diseases had been lumped under the general heading of distemper. In the last few years modern science has isolated a number of separate diseases of the distemper complex, such as infectious hepatitis, hard-pad disease, influenza, and primary encephalitis, which had been diagnosed as distemper. Thus, with more accurate diagnosis, great strides have been made in conquering not only distemper, but these other, allied diseases. Distemper (Carre) is now rare, due to successful methods of immuni-

227

zation, but any signs of illness in an animal not immunized may be the beginning of the disease. The symptoms are so similar to those of various other diseases that only a trained observer can diagnose correctly. Treatment consists of the use of drugs to counteract complications arising from the invasion of secondary diseases and in keeping the stricken animal warm, well fed, comfortable and free from dehydration until the disease has run its course. In many instances, even if the pup gets well, he will be left with some dreadful souvenir of the disease which will mar him for life. After-effects are common in most of the diseases of the distemper complex.

The tremendous value of immunization against this viral disease cannot be exaggerated. Except for the natural resistance your animal carries against disease, it is the one means of protection you have against this killer. There have been various methods of immunization developed in the last several years, but it would seem that the most recently favored is the avianized vaccine (or chick embryo-adapted vaccine). There are reasonably sure indications that this avianized vaccine protects against hard-pad disease and primary encephalitis as well as distemper. Injections can be given at any age,

Much natural protection for the puppies has been passed on by the mother; however, as soon as the puppies are six weeks old, it is time to take them to the veterinarian for their initial inoculations.

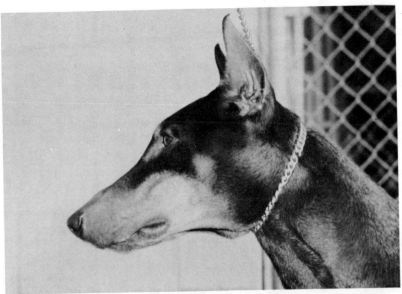

This Doberman is an example of excellent health, and with little doubt will remain so, because the owners keep abreast of developments in modern veterinary medicine, and then give their champion the protection he deserves.

even as early as six or eight weeks, with a repeat dosage at six months of age. It does not affect the tissues, nor can it cause any ill effects to other dogs who come in contact with the vaccinated animal.

Infectious hepatitis

This disease attacks dogs of all ages, but is particularly deadly to puppies. We see young puppies in the nest, healthy, bright and sturdy; suddenly they begin to vomit, and the next day they are dead of infectious hepatitis—it strikes that quickly. The disease is almost impossible to diagnose correctly, and there is no known treatment that will cure it. Astute authorities claim that if an afflicted dog survives three days after the onslaught of the disease he will, in all probability, completely recover.   Research has given us a vaccine that affords safe and effective protection against infectious hepatitis.

Rabies

This is the most terrible of diseases, since it knows no bounds. It is transmissible to all kinds of animals and birds, including the superior animal, man. To contract this dread disease, the dog must be bitten by a rabid animal or the rabies virus must enter the body through a broken skin surface. The disease incubation period is governed by the distance of the virus point of entry to the brain. The closer the point of entry is to the brain, the quicker the disease manifests itself. We can be thankful that rabies is not nearly as prevalent as is supposed by the uninformed. Restlessness, excitability, perverted appetite, character reversal, wildness, drowsiness, loss of acuteness of senses, (and of feeling, in some instances) foaming at the mouth, and many other lesser symptoms come with the onslaught of this disease. Diagnosis by trained persons of a portion of the brain is conceded to be the only way of determining whether an animal died of rabies or of one of the distemper complex diseases. Very little has been done in introducing drugs or specifics that can give satisfaction in combating this disease; perhaps evaluation of the efficacy of such products is almost impossible with a disease so rare and difficult to diagnose.

In 1948 an avianized, modified live virus vaccine was found, and is being used throughout this country today. Quarantine, such as that pursued in England, even of six months' duration, is still not the answer to the rabies question, though it is undeniably

The bright eyes of this Doberman indicate his health and vigor.

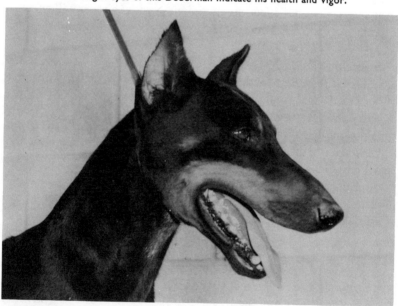

230

A healthy Doberman is an active Doberman.

effective. It is, however, not proof positive. Recently a dog on arriving in England was held in quarantine for the usual six months. The day before he was to be released to his owners, the attendant noticed that he was acting strangely. He died the next day. Under examination his brain showed typical inclusion bodies, establishing the fact that he had died of rabies. This is a truly dangerous disease that can bring frightful death to animal or man. With an effective way of immunization known and recommended by authoritative sources, it should be the duty of every dog owner to protect his dog, himself, his family, and neighbors from even the slight risk that exists of contracting rabies by taking immediate advantage in this form of protection.

FITS

Fits in dogs are symptoms of diseases rather than illness itself. They can be caused by the onslaught of any number of diseases, including worms, distemper, epilepsy, primary encephalitis, poisoning, etc. Running fits can also be traced to dietary deficiencies. The underlying reason for the fits, or convulsions, must be diagnosed by your veterinarian and the cause treated.

DIARRHEA

Diarrhea, which is officially defined as watery movements occurring eight or more times a day, is often a symptom of one of many other diseases. But, if on taking your dog's temperature, you find there is no fever, it is quite possible the condition has been caused by either a change of diet, of climate or water, or even by a simple intestinal disturbance. A tightening agent such as Kaopectate should be given. Water should be withheld and corn syrup, dissolved in boiled milk, substituted to prevent dehydration in the patient. Feed hard-boiled eggs, boiled milk, meat, cheese, boiled white rice, cracker, kibbles, or dog biscuits. Add a tablespoonful of bone ash (not bone meal) to the diet. If the condition is not corrected within two or three days, if there is an excess of blood passed in the stool, or if signs of other illness become manifest, don't delay a trip to your veterinarian.

CONSTIPATION

If the dog's stool is so hard that it is difficult for him to pass it and he strains and grunts during the process, then he is obviously con-

A Doberman's ears should be cropped by the time he is eight weeks old. The veterinarian puts the dog under anesthesia so that the operation is painless.

Both mother and puppy are in excellent health because they have received proper food, care, housing, and medical attention when needed.

stipated. The cause of constipation is diet. Bones and dog biscuits, given abundantly, can cause this condition, as can any of the items of diet mentioned above as treatment for diarrhea. Chronic constipation can result in hemorrhoids which, if persistent, must be removed by surgery. The cure for constipation and its accompanying ills is the introduction of laxative food elements into the diet. Stewed tomatoes, buttermilk, skim milk, whey, bran, alfalfa meal, and various fruits can be fed and a bland physic given. Enemas can bring quick relief. Once the condition is rectified, the dog should be given a good balanced diet, avoiding all types of foods that will produce constipation.

EYE AILMENTS

The eyes are not only the mirror of the soul, they are also the mirror of many kinds of disease. Discharge from the eyes is one of the many symptoms warning of most internal viral, parasitic, and bacterial diseases. Of the ailments affecting the eye itself, the most usual are: glaucoma, which seems to be a hereditary disease; pink eye, a strep infection; cataracts; opacity of the lens in older dogs; corneal

233

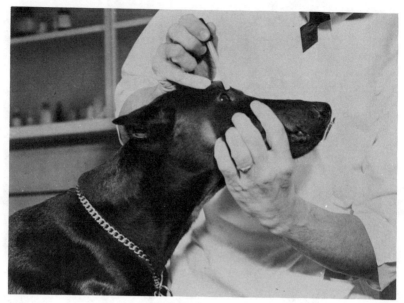
Unless it is an irritation caused by dust, wind, or sand, let your veterinarian treat your Doberman's eyes.

opacity, such as follows some cases of infectious hepatitis; and teratoma. Mange, fungus, inturned lids, and growths on the lid are other eye ailments. The wise procedure is to consult your veterinarian for specific treatment.

When the eyes show a discharge from reasons other than those that can be labeled "ailment", such as irritation from dust, wind, or sand, they should be washed with warm water on cotton or a soft cloth. After gently washing the eyes, an ophthalmic ointment combining a mild anesthetic and antiseptic can be utilized. Butyl sulphate, 1 percent yellow oxide of mercury, and 5 percent sulphathiazole ointment are all good. Boric acid seems to be falling out of favor as an opthalmic antiseptic. The liquid discharged by the dog's tear ducts is a better antiseptic, and much cheaper.

ANAL GLANDS

If your male dog consistently drags his rear parts on the ground or bites this area, the cause is probably impacted anal glands. These glands, which are located on each side of the anus, should be periodically cleared by squeezing. The job is not a nice one, and can be much more effectively done by your veterinarian. Unless these glands are kept reasonably clean, infection can become housed in this site, resulting in the formation of an abscess which will need surgical care. Dogs that get an abundance of exercise seldom need the anal glands attended to.

The many other ailments which your dog is heir to, such as cancer, tumors, rupture, heart disease, fractures, and the results of accidents, must all be diagnosed and tended to by your veterinarian. When you go to your veterinarian with a sick dog, always remember to bring along a sample of his stool for analysis. Many times samples of his urine are needed, too. Your veterinarian is the only one qualified to treat your dog for disease, but protection against disease is to a great extent in the hands of the dog owner. If those hands are capable, a great deal of pain and misery for both dog and owner can be eliminated. Death can be cheated, investment saved, and veterinary bills kept to a minimum. A periodic health check by your veterinarian is a wise investment.

ADMINISTERING MEDICATION

Some people seem to have ten thumbs on each hand when they attempt to give medicine to their dog. They become agitated and

Every puppy's health is in his owner's hands.

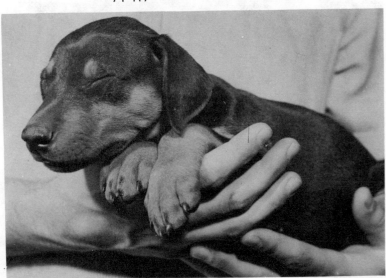

approach the task with so little sureness that their mood is communicated to the patient, increasing the difficulties. Invite calmness and quietness in the patient by emanating these qualities yourself. Speak to the animal in low, easy tones, petting him slowly, quieting him down in preparation. The administration of medicine should be made without fuss and as though it is some quiet and private new game between you and your dog.

At the corner of your dog's mouth there is a lip pocket perfect for the administering of liquid medicine if used correctly. Have the animal sit, then raise his muzzle so that his head is slanted upward looking toward the sky. Slide two fingers in the corner of his mouth where the upper and lower lip edges join, pull gently outward, and you have a pocket between the cheek flesh and the gums. Into this pocket pour the liquid medicine slowly. Keep his head up, and the liquid will run from the pocket into his throat and he will swallow it. Continue this procedure until the complete dose has been given. This will be easier to accomplish if the medicine has been spooned into a small bottle. The bottle neck, inserted into the lip pocket, is tipped, and the contents will slowly run down his throat.

This is another way to give your dog a capsule. Place the capsule as far back on the base of the tongue as possible. Withdraw your hand quickly and close the Doberman's mouth.

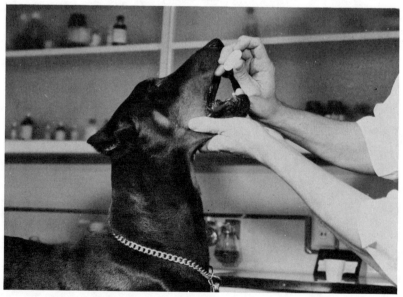

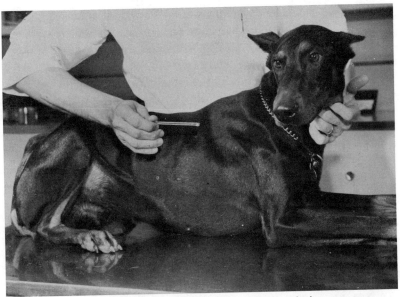
An ordinary rectal thermometer can be used to take your dog's temperature.

To give pills or capsules, the head of the patient must again be raised with muzzle pointing upward. With one hand, grasp the cheeks of the pup just behind the lip edges where the teeth come together on the inside of the mouth. With the thumb on one side and the fingers on the other, press inward as though squeezing. The lips are pushed against the teeth, and the pressure of your fingers forces the mouth open. The dog will not completely close his mouth, since doing so would cause him to bite his lips. With your other hand, insert the pill in the patient's mouth as far back on the base of the tongue as you can, pushing it back with your second finger. Withdraw your hand quickly, allow the dog to close his mouth, and hold it closed with your hand, but not too tightly. Massage the dog's throat and watch for the tip of his tongue to show between his front teeth, signifying the fact that the capsule or pill has been swallowed.

In taking your dog's temperature, an ordinary rectal thermometer is adequate. It must be first shaken down, then dipped in vaseline, and inserted into the rectum for approximately three-quarters of its length. Allow it to remain there for no less than a full minute, restraining the dog from sitting during that time. When withdrawn, it should be wiped with a piece of cotton, read, then washed in alcohol—never hot water. The arrow on most thermometers at 98.6 degrees indicates normal human temperature and should be disregarded. Normal temperature for your grown dog is 101 degrees; normal dog temperature varies between $101\frac{1}{2}$ and 102 degrees. Excitement can raise the temperature, so it is best to take a reading only when the dog is calm.

In applying an ophthalmic ointment to the eye, simply pull the lower lid out, squeeze a small amount of ointment into the pocket thus produced, and release the lid. The dog will blink, and the ointment will spread over the eye.

Should you find it necessary to give your dog an enema, employ an ordinary human-size bag and rubber hose. Simply grease the catheter with vaseline and insert the hose well into the rectum. The bag should be held high for a constant flow of water. A quart of warm soapy water or plain water with a tablespoonful of salt makes an efficient enema for a big dog. Puppies need proportionately less.

FIRST AID

Emergencies quite frequently occur which make it necessary for you to care for the dog yourself until veterinary aid is available.

Whenever first aid is required for a severe cut, apply a pressure bandage to stop bleeding, and then take your dog to your veterinarian.

One way to protect your Doberman from unnecessary accidents is to keep him on a leash while not kenneled or in the home.

Quite often emergency help by the owner can save the pup's life or lessen the chance of permanent injury. A badly injured animal, blinded to all else but abysmal pain, often reverts to the primitive, wanting only to be left alone with his misery. Injured, panic-stricken, not recognizing you, he might attempt to bite when you wish to help him. Under the stress of fright and pain, this reaction is normal in animals. A muzzle can easily be slipped over his foreface, or a piece of bandage or strip of cloth can be fashioned into a muzzle by looping it around the dog's muzzle, crossing it under the jaws, and bringing the two ends around in back of the dog's head and tying them. Snap a leash onto his collar as quickly as possible to prevent him from running away and hiding. If it is necessary to lift him, grasp him by the neck, getting as large a handful of skin as you can, as high up on the neck as possible. Hold tight and he won't be able to turn his head far enough around to bite. Lift him off the ground by the hold you have on his neck, encircle his body with your other arm, and support him or carry him.

Every dog owner should have handy a first-aid kit specifically for the use of his dog. It should contain a thermometer, surgical scissors, rolls of three-inch and six-inch bandage, a roll of one-inch adhesive tape, a package of surgical cotton, a jar of vaseline, enema equipment, bulb syringe, ten c.c. hypodermic syringe, flea powder, skin remedy, tweezers, ophthalmic ointment, paregoric, Kaopectate, peroxide of hydrogen, merthiolate, Army Formula Foot Powder, alcohol, ear remedy, aspirin, milk of magnesia, castor oil, mineral oil, and dressing salve.

Here are two charts for your reference, one covering general first-aid measures and the other a chart of poisons and antidotes. Remember that in most instances these are emergency measures, not specific treatments, and are designed to help you in aiding your dog until you can reach your veterinarian.

FIRST-AID CHART

Emergency	Treatment	Remarks
Accidents	Automobile, treat for shock. If gums are white, indicates probable internal injury. Wrap bandage tightly around body until it forms a sheath. Keep very quiet until veterinarian comes.	Call veterinarian immediately.

Both owner and Doberman can put their trust in a competent veterinarian.

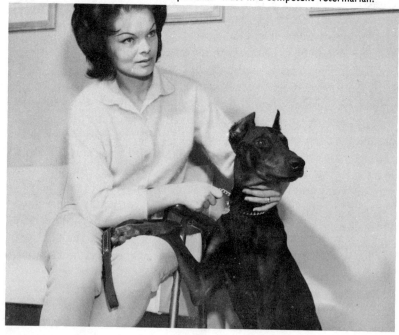

Bee stings	Give paregoric or aspirin to ease pain. If in state of shock, treat for same.	Call veterinarian for advice.
Bites (animal)	Tooth wounds—area should be shaved and antiseptic solution flowed into punctures, with eye dropper. Iodine, merthiolate, etc., can be used. If badly bitten or ripped, take dog to your veterinarian for treatment.	If superficial wounds become infected after first aid, consult veterinarian.
Bloat	Stomach distends like a balloon. Pierce stomach wall with hollow needle to allow gas to escape. Follow with stimulant—2 cups of coffee.	
Burns	Apply strong, body heat strained tea to burned area, followed by covering of vaseline.	Unless burn is very minor, consult veterinarian immediately.
Broken bones	If break involves a limb, fashion splint to keep immobile. If ribs, pelvis, shoulder, or back involved, keep dog from moving until professional help comes.	Call veterinarian immediately.
Choking	If bone, wood, or any foreign object can be seen at back of mouth or throat remove with fingers. If object can't be removed or is too deeply imbedded or too far back in throat, rush to veterinarian immediately.	.
Cuts	Minor cuts: allow dog to lick and cleanse. If not within his reach, clean cut with peroxide, then apply merthiolate. Severe cuts: apply pressure bandage to stop bleeding—a wad of bandage over wound and bandage wrapped tightly over it. Take to veterinarian.	If cut becomes infected or needs suturing, consult veterinarian.
Dislocations	Keep dog quiet and take to veterinarian at once.	
Drowning	Artificial respiration. Lay dog on his side, push with hand on his ribs, release quickly. Repeat every 2 seconds. Treat for shock.	

241

Electric shock	Artificial respiration. Treat for shock.	Call veterinarian immediately.
Heat stroke	Quickly immerse the dog in cold water until relief is given. Give cold water enema. Or lay dog flat and pour cold water over him, turn electric fan on him, and continue pouring cold water as it evaporates.	Cold towel pressed against abdomen aids in reducing temp. quickly if quantity of water not available.
Porcupine quills	Tie dog up, hold him between knees, and pull all quills out with pliers. Don't forget tongue and inside of mouth.	See veterinarian to remove quills too deeply imbedded.
Shock	Cover dog with blanket. Administer stimulant (coffee with sugar). Allow him to rest, and soothe with voice and hand.	Alcoholic beverages are NOT stimulants.
Snake bite	Cut deep X over fang marks. Drop potassium-permanganate into cut. Apply tourniquet above bite if on foot or leg.	Apply first aid only if a veterinarian or a doctor can't be reached.

POISON	HOUSEHOLD ANTIDOTE
ACIDS	Bicarbonate of soda
ALKALIES (cleansing agents)	Vinegar or lemon juice
ARSENIC	Epsom salts
HYDROCYANIC ACID (wild cherry; laurel leaves)	Dextrose or corn sirup
LEAD (paint pigments)	Epsom salts
PHOSPHORUS (rat poison)	Peroxide of hydrogen
MERCURY	Eggs and milk
THEOBROMINE (cooking chocolate)	Phenobarbital
THALLIUM (bug poisons)	Table salt in water
FOOD POISONING (garbage, etc.)	Peroxide of hydrogen, followed by enema
STRYCHNINE	Sedatives. Phenobarbital, Nembutal.
DDT	Peroxide and enema

The important thing to remember when your dog is poisoned is that prompt action is imperative. Administer an emetic immediately. Mix hydrogen peroxide and water in equal parts. Force

A divider can keep a puppy out of all kinds of trouble around the house.

A heart examination is in order for older Dobermans.

this mixture down your dog. In a few minutes he will regurgitate his stomach contents. Once this has been accomplished, call your veterinarian. If you know the source of the poison and the container which it came from is handy, you will find the antidote on the label. Your veterinarian will prescribe specific drugs and advise on their use.

The symptoms of poisoning include trembling, panting, intestinal pain, vomiting, slimy secretion from mouth, convulsions, coma. All these symptoms are also prevalent in other illnesses, but if they appear and investigation leads you to believe that they are the result of poisoning, act with dispatch as described above.

INDEX

Helios v. Siegestor, 20
Hemorrhoids, 233
Hepatitis, infectious, 227, 229, 234
Heredity, 35-41
Hernia, 85
Hindquarters, 30-31, 33
Hips, 27
Hock, *illus.*, 30
Hock joint, *illus.*, 30
Hocks, 33
Holland, history of the Doberman in, 16
Home doctoring, 195
Homemade dinner, 102-103
Hookworms, 212-213, 223
    larvae infection, 222
Hound glove, 168
Housebreaking, 117-121
Housing, 151-162
    in apartments, 153
Huskies, 13
Hydrocyanic acid, poisoning, 242
Hydrogen peroxide, 215, 240, 241, 242
Hypodermic syringe, 240

I

Inbreeding, 39, 40-41
Incisors, 84
Inclusion bodies, 231
Indoor sleeping quarters, 157-159
Infected navel, 88
Infectious hepatitis, 227, 229, 234
Inheritance, 36-39
Influenza, 227
Internal parasites, 205-206
Intestinal pain, 244
Inturned lids, 234
Iodine, 99, 241
Iron, 99
Isabella color, 47
Italy, 16

J

Jaeger, 20
Jessy v.d. Sonnenhoehe, 21
Judging, 33
Jumping on people, 133

K

Kaopectate, 155, 232
Kennels, 155
    outdoor, 154
    professional, 154
    runs, and bedding, 151-162
Kerosene, 185, 186
Kibble, 107
    with meal and vegetables, 105

L

Labor
    contractions, 69
    signs of trouble, 72
Large litters, 71
Lead poisoning, 242
Lead training, 127-128
Legs, 30
    swelling of, 211, 212
Lemon juice, 242
Leptospirosis, 233, 234
    and rats, 224
Lice, 182, 199, 223
Lie down! 130
Life span, 51
Line breeding, 39, 41
Linseed oil, 98
Liquid medicine, administering, 236
Litters, large, 71
Liver, 102
Lockjaw, 223, 225
Loin, *illus.*, 30
Loins, 27, 33
Loose stool, 225 (see also Diarrhea)
Loss of acuteness of senses, 230
Loss of appetite, 209, 212, 219, 226
Loss of weight, 212
Lower thigh, *illus.*, 30
Luteal bodies, 58
Luteal hormone, 58
Lysol, 157

M

Magnesium, 99
Major win, 32
Malucidin, 221
Manchester Terrier, 14, 21, 41, 47